T0196903

I am Avatar

∞

You are Avatar

Michelle Stone

BALBOA.
PRESS
A DIVISION OF HAY HOUSE

Balboa Press books may be ordered through booksellers or by contacting:

Balboa Press
A Division of Hay House
1663 Liberty Drive
Bloomington, IN 47403
www.balboapress.com
1 (877) 407-4847

Because of the dynamic nature of the Internet, any web addresses or links contained in this book may have changed since publication and may no longer be valid. The views expressed in this work are solely those of the author and do not necessarily reflect the views of the publisher, and the publisher hereby disclaims any responsibility for them.

The author of this book does not dispense medical advice or prescribe the use of any technique as a form of treatment for physical, emotional, or medical problems without the advice of a physician, either directly or indirectly. The intent of the author is only to offer information of a general nature to help you in your quest for emotional and spiritual well-being. In the event you use any of the information in this book for yourself, which is your constitutional right, the author and the publisher assume no responsibility for your actions.

Any people depicted in stock imagery provided by Thinkstock are models, and such images are being used for illustrative purposes only.
Certain stock imagery © Thinkstock.

Print information available on the last page.

ISBN: 978-1-5043-8494-0 (sc)
ISBN: 978-1-5043-8493-3 (hc)
ISBN: 978-1-5043-8495-7 (e)

Library of Congress Control Number: 2017911594

Balboa Press rev. date: 08/08/2017

In honour of and dedicated to:

*The one who has sought Truth, meaning in brokenness
and the Divine within the ordinary.*

To the one who has sought a miracle.

*To the one who desires intimacy within and with another and thus
desires to answer the call and potential of their soul: to see and be
seen. You are of Love and of Love you are destined to become.*

*To the one who believes in a spiritual path, purpose, and potential
and is relentless in their search for another way of being.*

*And thus, this book is dedicated to the one who desires
to fully become the being they were destined to be...*

You are the one of the One; you are the greatest one.

Man's greatest desire was and remains to see and be seen in the totality and truth of all that he is; truly Divine. He is of Divine purpose, potential and nature. Man desires not a miracle but rather a world in which he can truly be free: to love and to be loved.

Avatar:
a manifestation of a deity or released soul in bodily
form on Earth, a Divine teacher on Earth.

∞ Preface ∞
The Present Day: The State of Play...

People seek a spiritual experience, a defining or life altering experience that will truly make the unknown known and the hidden revealed. Yet, in this state of constant search, *the spiritual* is treated as an elusive concept that always remains slightly out of reach. For many, hiding has become an acceptable and unyielding existence. 'Nobody's perfect' and 'I'm only human' have become commonplace statements and perhaps excuses for failure to accept responsibility for one's actions, behaviour and one's conscious evolution.

Nonetheless, the hunger to be truly seen and known compels and drives the individual forward. Belief and hope are the sustenance that sustains the soul when the shallow existence fails and life crumbles unapologetically around you. In moments of deep despair, one only has the sanctuary of one's own soul and whilst others are willing witnesses and compassionate companions...it remains that one must truly face himself alone.

Yet, the spiritual remains ever-present because the deepest place within is always accessible. One needs not a miracle, rather one needs a shift in one's way of being. One must come to know himself as small in his understanding of all that happens within and around him and as if almost paradoxical...one must also know himself as powerful beyond measure. Man, must come to know himself as he truly is; of Divine purpose, potential and nature. He is connected to all that was, all that is and all that is yet to be revealed. He holds influence and he is powerful. In honour of the Divinity within and above, the spiritual space within must be made manifest in all peoples, places, and encounters.

Man, must commence the journey in the full knowledge that he knows little, is willing to learn and from this place of innocent trust he will yield the dividend beyond dividends; he will come to truly know the Divine within and above. Innocent trust will become surefooted knowledge and wisdom will be his due reward. He will be wise in both his knowingness and his unknowingness.

Man, must learn to observe his own experience of every given moment with a sense of wonder and search for the deeper meaning, purpose and potential in all peoples, places, and experiences. This desire will be duly rewarded. Man, will see himself as more than a mere human and thus come to know himself as he is in truth: a spiritual deity. Man, must engage with life from the deepest place within him and allow himself to be truly seen, for beyond the drama and beyond the story, he is only of love. Thus, he must release himself from himself and trust his heart, for his heart truly knows and love truly is…

Man, must seek the magical and mystical in all that is and be satisfied in the knowledge that whilst he knows much, he also knows little. He must allow the Divine to work His hand in and around him. He must be the willing victim and thus the worthy victor.

He must find and allow that place within that truly knows and truly sees to guide his light, life, and actions. In the knowledge that his understanding is truly incomplete, he is open to finding himself again and again. Thus, he will always be redefining himself and his experience.

From this space of perfect imperfection, he will come to know himself as he truly is; always in a state of flux and flow. He will desire his own destiny and be open to allowing his gifts within to be made manifest in the world. He will be humbled by his own talents as he will know that they are of the Divine and as he has been gifted, he will gift others. He will find the Divine spark within and become a creative being, joyous that he is of the Divine and that his potential and purpose are being made manifest to their perfect potential in the world.

He will be creative and destiny will be his path. Rather than perpetuating a hidden existence, he will show up as he truly is and is destined to be...He will be spiritual and the desired unknown will become the known...He will see and be seen; of love, he is and of love he is destined to become.

∞ Acknowledgement ∞

In honour of the inspired scribe, whose compulsion to record the teachings of the Avatar gifted many eons ago.

He believed in the unseen and was inspired by the unknown.

As he was inspired, he will inspire many; his legacy is your destiny.

∞ Introduction ∞

It was and always remains so that the
unknown can be revered or feared.

And thus, many silently desired the spiritual existence or the peak experience. As they hid their inner landscape from themselves and another, their varied inner worlds held one unified desire; they collectively desired to be truly seen and truly known. They desired to connect with themselves and another. They wanted to understand within and around. They wanted to truly know that there was more than their limited human experiencing. They wanted to be spiritual beings.

They searched and searched and yet *the spiritual* remained slightly obscure. Whilst they knew, they did not truly know, for if they were as powerful as contended then the humble human was as much to be revered as feared. And thus, in their silent desire they were connected and their collective call was so fervent and unrelenting that the Divine answered in a way that both assured and challenged them...

Eons ago, in the year that was, a bright light appeared steadfast in the sky. It sat between the moon and stars and beside the sun. It remained there for many a day and night. The multitudes gathered to curiously observe the bright light. Unfortunately, their curiosity became frustrated unknowingness. 'Twas as if the initially termed *'miracle'* was becoming ordinary...many still desired to see and know more. The sceptics departed and the firm believers remained. The seekers were overcome with confirmation and affirmation of their faith. Their investment and reverence in the unknown was duly rewarded as on the thirty third day a being emerged from the light. He looked exactly like them only he emanated a bright light. He was in their world but not of their world. He bore the name *Avatar.*

It is said that he told them all they would need to know and if they truly listened they would truly understand. He argued that Truth deemed no elaborations or embellishments and thus he was brief and concise in his teachings. The rule of communication was simple; listen from your soul. Their reward for listening would render them forever changed and thus whilst they feared him, they also desired his presence.

Fortunately, one soul as if inspired documented the teachings of the Avatar. The delicate manuscript survived the intermittent centuries and was uncovered in an unlikely place. The pages forth are the reproduction of this manuscript. No amendments have been made and thus the manuscript remains in its truest and purest form. The mass reproduction of this manuscript honours both the known and the unknown and is done so in the belief that as many silently desired the spiritual before, many silently desire the spiritual now and as the Divine answered this call eons ago, the Divine has answered this call again today in the pages set forth.

The manuscript presented in the pages ahead is an exact replication of the inspired scribe's manuscript of the teachings of the Avatar. His name was not found on the manuscript. Perhaps it was destined to be so, that he would be unknown in his name and only revealed in his legacy: this manuscript. The decision to replicate this manuscript was to honour his action then, and as he shared before, he shares again. Perhaps it was a moment of defined destiny that his hidden manuscript would be revealed again today.

Thus, the words in this book commence belonging to no-one and accordingly you are afforded the opportunity to make them yours. You found this book or perhaps this book found you. The words of this book can belong to you, for as you read them, they will touch the essence of your being and meet the stirrings of your soul. You will be forever transformed as you allow this book to move you.

In the contemporary world, today, many books are available to those who seek an answer, a solution, or a remedy for the soul. Perhaps, this original manuscript directly or indirectly inspired present, and past authors. Perhaps these authors were descendants of the ones who directly listened to the Avatar centuries ago, or descendants of the ones who were bestowed the opportunity to read the inspired scribe's manuscript. This is not beyond the realms of possibility and accordingly it remains a distinct possibility that this is the original book from which many others were distilled.

As you read the ancient word of the Avatar, you will see that he speaks in a concise and brief manner. Thus, one learns that Truth in its purest form requires no elaborations or embellishments. Truth simply just is. The language of the soul requires no extended narrative. Language is powerful when used for its' original purpose; to reveal and understand oneself and another.

The words of the Avatar are spiritual alone and thus they seek to meet the spiritual space within you. Perhaps his words are powerful, for they effortlessly break through your invisible walls and unnecessary defences and touch you. Thus, he guides you to the deepest part of you, in honour that the unknown within you may become known, that the answer you seek might be found.

The Avatar speaks of you, of life, and all that is and effortlessly extends you the opportunity to transform or redefine your existence, that you might become all that you are destined to be. Perhaps it may only be a word, a sentence, an excerpt, or the manuscript in its entirety that catches you, touches you or moves you and thus you have found the deepest place within you. Thus, a gift in the waiting lies in this manuscript for you.

The Avatar holds an unequivocal ability to speak to the spiritual alone. He landed only of light and of light he remained. As the humans, then and the humans now reverently desire the spiritual path or the way of light, he offers his word and his wisdom to you in the moment that is now, that you might find what you reverently seek within you; the spiritual. He offers his word that you might review and rework your experiences and come to understand the deeper meaning, purpose, and potential of all that has happened to you in the moments past and the moments unknown. The Avatar teaches for you to learn and know yourself and all that is as spiritual.

As you so desired, your call is now answered and in the waiting, lies a moment of great making. May you feel the power within his word and thus, the power within you. May the word of the Avatar breathe into your being and from the deepest part of you, may you come to know you, another and all that is...as spiritual.

May you be forever transformed as the words of the Avatar touch you, soothe you, move you, inspire you and compel you. The words in the waiting have the potential to gift you; words known in the soul can never be unknown. His word will always lie within you.

May his teachings become your learning, as the meanings you take from his words become your own individual understandings. Thus, may you be rendered forever changed by your own individual encounter with the Avatar in the pages ahead.

He is waiting for you, for he knew you would come, the reason for your coming now irrelevant, for the call of destiny lies in the moment that is now. The potential of the present moment is now profound for you are about to be transformed by your encounter with the Avatar. Your heart wide open or closed, he will touch you, such is his power and his magnificence.

His word is ancient and yet beautifully relevant today. Truth simply stands alone and simply just is. May you come to know you anew: in Truth alone: of love, you are and of love alone you are destined to become. It was only a matter of time...

You are the one of the One;
you are the greatest one.

∞ ∞ ∞ ∞ ∞

∞ A Message from the Inspired Scribe ∞

The Avatar landed in a way unknown, in a land far away from his spiritual home. Although he looked like them, they knew he was special. The humans were perplexed. Thought and talk was rampant. Who is this being who looks like us but behaves in ways unknown? I don't know whether to call him foreigner or friend? In his physical appearance, I see myself; he has a body like mine, yet his presence is indefinable. It's in his eyes, the way he moves with an ease of grace and when he opens his mouth, there is a wisdom carried upon a wave of effortless expression.

I ask myself, where does his wisdom come from? The thoughts he expresses are gentle reminders, resonating within me. I cannot describe it for to limit my experiencing of him in words would surrender him to a definable place and injustice would enter. I realise that whilst he challenges me, I also know he speaks the Truth and his Truth whispers relentlessly to my own inner knowing.

In a moment of exasperation, I realised with haste-I hold a Divine duty to propagate the wisdom of the Avatar. I must validate his presence through the documentation of his teachings. Thus, humankind now and forthcoming can be enlightened.

Whilst the words I write will never fully encapsulate the entirety of the experience of meeting this entity, it is the only way that this wisdom may be shared. For so, I have been gifted, I can gift you also.

In an authoritative voice, the Avatar shares, "I consent to your request to write my word, in the aspiration that others will be inspired. I hold only one stipulation prior to my engagement, you must scribe my teachings in their truest form. Your own descriptions or experiences of me cease at this point, for these are exactly that: your own. Others who read must come to make their own understanding of my word; it must touch them in its purest form only. So, cease the sharing of your own understanding and so it shall naturally follow that others are gifted the gift of their own understanding. I feel a tear arise in my eye as this should not be so, as one's own understanding should never be bestowed but should arise from one's own inner knowingness within. Nonetheless, this is the experiencing that is on Earth and we must start from this moment forth to create a new way".

From this point, forth, in the pages ahead, I am a mere scribe. You will meet the Avatar in his words alone. Your encounter with the Avatar is exactly that-your encounter with the Avatar. He speaks directly to you; to your heart, to your spirit, to your soul and should you so desire may you be forever changed by your encounter with the Avatar.

The
Teachings of
The Avatar

∞

1

∞ I am Avatar...You are Avatar ∞

My name 'Avatar' is from Sanskrit. 'Avatára' is derived from the blending of 'ava' meaning 'down' and 'tar' meaning 'to cross'. My opinion on this definition is irrelevant. You must make your own of the name I hold. Having definitions of my name may allow you to relate to me and to understand me. Only for this reason, do I share the definition.

I begin my wisdom, where you began; your birth. One's birth is one of the most significant life events one will ever have. Your death is the other significant event. You share these two common experiences across the planet Earth with the billions of humans. Your birth-death commonality identified, another is a stranger no more. You were birthed in connection to: all who came before you, all who come with you and all who will come after you. From now on you must cease grappling with the abstract concept that you term connection, for now you have been told.

Your mortality is the finite space between your two significant life events of birth and death. Your mortality is finite in order that you may unleash your infinite potential. If your mortality was infinite, you run the threat of never becoming all that you are capable of becoming. Thus, your mortality hastens you to become all that you are destined to become in a definitive time. You were born with an inordinate potential. Have you unleashed your perfect potential in the world? What greatness lies within you? Who and what are you in the world?

Avatar meaning 'I came down to cross'...of the Divine I came and the land of man I shall cross. My time on the land of man is this a human experience or a spiritual experience? Your time on the land of man is this a human experience or a spiritual experience? Your answer to that very question will define your everything.

My name was first defined in Hinduism as a manifestation of a deity or released soul in bodily form on Earth, a Divine teacher on Earth. I was birthed as a manifestation of a deity. Deity meaning of Divine nature. You are also of a Divine nature. Obscured or known, it is so. My soul is released, as my Divine nature leads the path I walk. You too may become a liberated soul. Simply allow the spark of the Divine ever-present within to guide your path. In doing so, you are a Divine teacher to all who came before you, to all who come with you and to all who may come beyond you... You are Avatar.

I am Avatar

∞

You are Avatar.

2

∞ The Divinity within ∞

Did you ever consider where you came from? I tell you solemnly you're being here was no random act or mere coincidence. You were born with a spark of the Divine within you. The Divine desired that one day that spark would be kindled to become a blazing light of passion: steady, tamed, tapered and unquenchable.

This spark is ever-present; always within you. Maybe you know this spark of the Divine? Maybe you have allowed this spark to grow to become a light to guide your path? Or maybe you require another to testify to its' existence to enable you to begin to touch it? Wherever you are on your path of Divinity, you are somewhere. You are never lost.

Maybe like many others, the spark of the Divine within has become obscured or hidden under a veil of illusion? Illusion arises when one attaches the virtue of the soul to something unworthy of the virtue of the soul. Thus, in the absence of touching your inner Divinity and allowing it to guide you, you have an untapped force within that remains dormant.

Dormant, nonetheless it is existent and ready for engagement. The world as it is may have suppressed this force. The world may have negated its' responsibility to support you in becoming a released soul. Nonetheless, if you choose to do so, you may manifest the being that you are. Although this may be a difficult task, as fellow travellers on the path may be sparse, it is possible.

You owe it to yourself and you owe it to the Creator that gently placed this Divinity within you to manifest your Divinity. You owe it to all who came before, with and may come beyond you to manifest your Divinity. You are called to gift the world with you.

Please step forth and pay your debt to all
concerned and connected: please serve.

3
∞ The Bodily Form ∞

Your body is the mere vessel of your soul. Your bodily form is first identifiable by matters such as gender, size, and physique. The sole purpose of your body is to hold and carry your soul.

What is visible to the outsider is no matter, relative to the soul within. The bodily form allows you to express your soul in the world-the way you move, the way you speak, the words you use, the way you touch another, the hands that build the outer manifestations of your inner dreams and visions...All express you in the world; all are your soulful expressions in the world.

The bodily form also serves the soul. In feeling the wind on your face, your soul is nourished. In seeing the sunset, your soul is granted respite and reprieve from the day that has passed. In hearing the bird carrying the morning song, your soul becomes ignited to meet the day ahead. In the lover's touch, your soul is stroked and revitalised.

The primary force of your soulful expression in the world is the words you use to communicate with another. Words, although abstract, stir the meanings within to be a gentle affirmation of all that you are or a destructive force that harms the essence of your being. Words are powerful. Choose your words with discernment and deliberateness; ensure they are reflective of the deep expression within. Pause before you respond to another. Their words must travel to your soul, a path further than your mind. When another's words touch your soul, your response will be an utterance from the Divine within. It is pure and true.

I hear some humans on this Earth utter the eyes are the windows of the soul. In the eyes, the attraction to the soul of another is engaged. There is a silent knowingness between two. In my eyes, you see the potential of all that I am, you see my heart, you see my soul, you see my spirit and I in you.

Regarding reliability and deception, the soul is the most reliable judge of your experiences. Your soul will smile with contentment when you are on the right path; your soul will feel liberated and freedom will abound. The soul is and always will be the most reliable truth detector. The eyes may not remember, the mind will forget and the ear may not hear. The soul will know.

Honour your body as the vessel of
expression of your soul.

∞ A Divine Teacher ∞

When you live your life from your soul, in honour of the Deity within, you become a Divine teacher. You inspire others to live their lives as an extensive expression of their own Divinity. You honour the learning inherent from all who went before you. You engage with others around you to unleash your Divine potential and their Divine potential. Your presence now is the inheritance to all who come after you.

To be taught by another you must be willing to learn. Similarly, to teach another you must also firstly be willing to learn. Within every human encounter there is a space of potential between two people. As you hear these words and feel my presence, a space of potential exists between us. You must be open and the pathway to your soul clear. My words must touch your soul and you need to allow them to touch your soul. You are the gatekeeper of your soul; admittance is your Divine right.

To be a Divine teacher, you must first come to know the spark of Divinity within. I can't tell you what this experience might look like or feel like. Your touching of your Divinity within is as personal as personal could be. It is the most intimate of all relationships. The admittance of another, like me, into that space is unthinkable and a direct violation of your relationship to your Divinity within. There is no place within that space for another.

When you touch the Divinity within, you will simply just know. You will be exercising your most reliable form of intelligence; your inner knowingness. Gradually you will build trust within your relationship to the Divinity within. You will listen to yourself and hear the Divinity within. Then you must choose to act upon the wisdom sequestered from your soul. As you act upon that source of guidance, dividends will be yielded. With gradual consistence, you will see change and transformation within your life. As your relationship with yourself changes, it naturally follows that your relationship with others also changes. And so, by expansion your relationship with the world changes...The spark of the Divine within becomes a light to your path and a light to others.

As you learned, so you will teach.

5
∞ The Child ∞

The child remains close to the Earth. He dances and delights in all that is. His spirit is most pure. You may contemplate him as a neophyte with a lot to learn about the world and life. You are the one who may learn plenty from him. Whilst you contemplate him as one who has yet to learn, I tell you solemnly it is you that has a lot to unlearn.

The child is free and trusts with ease in all that is unknown. He walks with a blind faith, with an open hand and an open heart. He remains close to his soul. His reactions and responses are natural and are the purest form of soulful expression. Somehow, this spirit becomes dulled and obscured and this is no mystery.

The child was birthed into a world of lack of spirit; a world that did not fully support the release of his soul. The child's instinct within and Divine spark were not mirrored by his surroundings and thus he learned to not trust his own inner knowingness. Surely, it was to become so, how could it be any different?

For although he knew, those he placed his trust in did not validate his knowingness. Perhaps, these were his parents or other significant others, the teachers, the community, the society; all the humans of his land. Rather than support the release of his soul, individuals unknowingly suppressed his Divinity within.

You see, the child is close to Avatar, possibly closer than you. In his laughter, joy, and freedom the child is living from the Divine spark. Rather than supporting the emergence of a steady flame from the spark, life forged his forgetfulness of his Divine nature. He became the tribe, the group, the clan.

Every disappointment, every other disillusionment, every other memory failed to nourish your soul. Disenchantment forged forgetfulness and made you doubt your soul's presence: made you doubt the essence of your being. To survive, you became the clan. Your sense of wonder disconfirmed frequently until the moment came when it became easier to not dream, to not remember and to not believe. It was easier for this existence to be so.

How might this have been if the tribe were in touch with their Divinity? Recognised and honoured their responsibility to support the release of the child's soul? You see the possibility of disservice to the child? Remember your child within, for he holds the makings of your joy, love, and freedom.

Unlearn to become.

∞ Parents ∞

If you so desire to become a parent or are a parent, remember the task implicitly implied in parenting. Your role is to support the child in releasing his soul. In supporting the release of his soul, you honour the potential of your own soul. You are a Divine Teacher to your child. You must support the evolution of his soul.

You must build your own inner knowingness on solid ground in order that you might nourish your child to become his own master. You must understand the task you undertake and the magnitude of influence that you hold, that you must direct wisely.

You must feed your child's soul through love, understanding and the impartment of knowledge. You must also gently challenge your child so that he might grow. You must model so that he might come to know the possibility of wisdom, truth and honour. You must teach him virtue.

You must trust yourself, so that he might learn to trust himself. You must allow him to be just so; him within the confinements of virtue and not the parameters of societal rules and expectations. Virtue as a guide is a compass that will serve him well, no matter where he finds himself.

Rather than become his own person, you must enable him to become his own soul. You are not required to show him the world; you are necessitated to show him the influence he holds within the world.

You must teach him in the knowledge and aspiration that one day he may become a parent or a Divine Teacher to his own children. Teach your child to trust all that is within him so that he may become all that he can be.

I am Avatar...you are Avatar...
your child will be Avatar.

Michelle Stone

∞ Potential ∞

Potential is as individual as individual could be. It is unique to your soul. You all hold potential. The manifestation of your potential in the world is the unique contribution to the evolution of all that you could make. Potential is the seed in hiding; obscured...you must search for the potential within.

How will I know the potential within? Potential can only be emancipated through challenge. Through challenge you must search within. Sometimes you must dig to the depths of you, to find all of you. You must find all that you are, to know all that you may become. Potential is only known with every step you take. You must step forward to know potential. It operates retrospectively; you must first act to know and then with acclaim you utter... 'I never knew I could do that'.

Courage precedes potential. You must first hold your courage to act. Fear attempts to annihilate your potential. However, fear can never destroy your potential. It may only hold your potential from rising. Sometimes, fear may only hold your potential momentarily. Sometimes, it may hold it for days to nights or for seasons to lifetimes. Irrespective of the captivation period, your potential is ever present.

Know that you are and always were destined for great things. Your potential for magnificence is undeniable. Like another you hold potential. Your greatness in the world is the manifestation of your potential. You have the potential to make a unique contribution to the world. A very special and precise gift that only you can bring. I say again...only you can bring.

Come to know thine own soul. In coming to know your soul, you will come to know the potential therein. No settling for mediocrity, for to do so is not humble. No quitting the quest for challenge, for to do so is the negating of your responsibility to your Self, Source, and all...

Manifest you in the world; manifest your potential.

You have the potential to bring forth a special
gift to the world. What's your gift?

∞ Purpose ∞

Purpose is closely connected to potential. Purpose and potential are Divine counterparts. Your life purpose stems from the seeds of potential within. What is the gift that you bring? What potential lies therein? What is your purpose?

Your purpose is to become a released soul; a manifestation of Divinity. How do you manifest Divinity in your life? Tell me the times when you are most Divine with your Self, with another, with all that is in this world...

In every moment, there is a choice to act with Divinity. From the Divine within, what are you choosing; light or darkness, compassion or judgement, to give or to withhold, separation or union? Are you one with Self and one with all?

Are you fit for the challenge? Can you hold courage in hand, act, release your potential and find your purpose? You must firstly bring purpose to all that you do. You must realise that in every task and every moment, there is a purpose. Quit searching and striving for purpose; first find the purpose in every given moment, in every given encounter and in every given task. All life is purpose from the mundane to exhilarating. The revelation of purpose in the moment, will lead you to find your life purpose.

When faced with a challenging situation, ask what's my purpose here? What is this given moment asking of me? What can

I bring to this situation? What can I do? What can I learn? How can I manifest my Divinity here? How can I act with purpose?

Start here, travel forth, and come to know your purpose in every given moment and the purpose of the moment will lead to the purpose of a lifetime. Now you know and so you shall act...

Your purpose is to live every given moment graciously,
in honour of the purpose placed therein.

Michelle Stone

∞ Truth ∞

Truth is just so. Those who live from the Divine within already know this; there is only one way. It either is or it isn't...it's that simple. When you touch your Divinity within and come to know that inner space of knowingness, then there is only one Truth.

In the very beginning, you knew the Truth. The Truth was close to you. You were close to the Avatar within. Those who live in Truth, live with the twinkle of a child in their eye. They know who they are: Divine. They trust that life truly gives. They trust the path, they trust the process and they trust themselves always. They know in Truth there is nothing to fear. They are where they are in any given moment, because destiny made it so.

Those who live in this manner did not stumble aimlessly upon Truth. Rather, at one exact moment in time, a desire for difference was birthed. They knew this wasn't the way it was meant to be and the time came when all the unyielding searching outside for the answer, forced them to search within.

At some point in your finite time, your moment will come and you will go within. Maybe many times before you have gone within and you have not ascribed this experience as such. Nonetheless, how do you think that you got to this perfect moment? Why do you hear my word at this moment in time, because you seek...you seek Truth?

You must hunger for Truth in your life and in all things. This hunger will sustain you and your spirit. Truth will lead to change in your life and in the lives of those you choose to share yourself with. Allow everyone and every experience to seek you out, to push you to own and expand your Truth. Experience will be both your teacher and your friend.

Trust you. Trust that there is only one abiding law in the governance of all: Truth. Decisions from a space of Truth are in alignment with the Divine for they arise from the Divinity within.

Truth in all things is just so. Seek, search, and strive for more; be a truth seeker. As life calls you, so you must answer. As your soul whispers, I desire to live in Truth only, all else will fall away. Shackles of illusion are exactly those shackles of illusion. Walk in Truth and be free to be all of who you are and all of who you are destined to become.

In all things, seek the Truth.

10

∞ Counsel ∞

Live in Truth and seek counsel if you must. Remember, in all things: first and foremost, seek counsel in yourself. Allow your Truth the space and opportunity to emerge. Seek counsel in the Divine always and should you be compelled to seek counsel in another, ensure that this other is an Elder more experienced than you; a wise authority, who also speaks from the Truth.

Truth within and above is ever-present. Yet, at times we may not be able to hear the Truth within and above. We do not engage the Elder to tell us the Truth. Rather, we engage the elder for the clarity he may have that in the given moment eludes us. The Elder's clarity enables us to find the ever-present Truth within again. The hidden is now revealed. The Elder exchange is then complete.

Remember this sentiment-When another approaches you in a state of confusion, desiring to find Truth to guide the path again. You do not give him the Truth. You enable him to clear the fog obscuring the emergence of his Truth. And thus, you enable his Truth to emerge. His Truth, remains so: his Truth.

Whilst you might explore options and choices, it is only him that will ultimately decide his path forward. This was and is his birth right. You allow him to find the rhythm of Truth within so that all his life and ways resonate again with the rhythm of Truth. Thus, one or many problems have been resolved through the attainment of clarity and once again he is free to walk his path in the tide of Truth.

You see Truth has an ever-present rhythm; the beating heart of one's Self and one's life. Those who walk with Truth are clear. They remain on good terms with themselves firstly. They relinquish all that is no longer in alignment with their Truth. Thus, they experience freedom. Freedom places a beat in their heart and a twinkle in their eye. They move with ease: grace.

Seek counsel in thyself first, in the Divine
always and with the Elder as guided.

∞ Responsibility ∞

All responsibility emerges from the soul. Your abiding responsibility in this lifetime is to become the released soul that you are destined to become: to become all you are destined to be. You must come to touch and know the Divinity within. Then, your Divine spark will become a Divine light. Your Divine light will illuminate your life, your path and all who traverse your path.

You were and are destined for greatness. You hold the responsibility to become this being of magnificence that moves with grace, in the strength of knowingness that all that went before was destined to be so and all that is yet to be revealed is the sweet mystery of the days ahead. You are indebted to yourself always and you owe it to you to become your greatness.

You are responsible for finding the Avatar within. I shine a light and signal the path but you must desire to walk the path. You must never walk the path for another, for this will diminish you. You must walk it for you. You are responsible for the destiny of your soul. You alone hold the responsibility to make the given moment an expression of all that it can be. You hold responsibility for the potential of your being and the potential of the moment therein.

What can you accomplish in this moment that might reflect your debt to your being and your debt to the Divine? How can you use this moment to express and manifest Divinity? You are responsible for your corner of the Earth. You must maintain your corner of the Earth with due diligence to all who came before you, all who come with you and all who may come beyond you. Treat this land and all herein with responsibility.

In choosing the path of Divinity, you will be called to challenge and denounce all that is not in accord with the Divine. You must answer the call when your name resounds. If you bear witness to misuse of one's position or authority, you must be willing to stand in the Truth. In this stance, you are rooted in and guided by the Divine to speak and act by whatever means necessary to challenge those who act in discord with Divinity, particularly when these actions are harmful to another. You act in such circumstances not from a space of retribution or superiority; you act from the space of Truth. To remain silent in the face of mistruth is to negate your responsibility to your being and the Divine. Treat it as an opportunity to brighten your light rather than dull your spark.

Be responsible: enable your Divine spark
to become a Divine light.

12

∞ Tenacity of Spirit ∞

Be tenacious in all you say and do. Tenacity is not a characteristic. It is more than mere self-belief. Tenacity is of a virtuous nature. Tenacity is of your spirit. It is a steadfast knowingness that you can encounter and overcome all. Your tenacity of spirit must be held with a sacred grace. It is a silent agreement between you and the Divine that together and in tandem with the life force that beats in your soul, you can overcome all that is.

The limiting precepts, beliefs or thoughts that arise in your head in times of strife are illusions. You must come to know and touch the given moment from the depths of your being: from your soul. When the soul leads the path, there is no place to give shelter to illusion. Truth prevails in all that is. You must remain tenacious and true to the larger Divinity that guides the Divinity within.

Challenge is aptly termed. Challenge arises to compel you to become all that you are and all you are destined to become. Treat challenge as your ally. Challenge forces you to shed all that no longer serves you. Challenge essentially means liberation. In challenge, you are called forth to become more Divine. Challenge always deems that you own and wear your tenacity of spirit. It is more than mere trust that all will subside. It is more than the mere sentiment that you will be okay. It is the depth of your being. It is ferocious in its' relentlessness to overcome the present moment, situation, or life event. It is the unyielding, non-compromising beast present in the Self that emerges from the depths to anchor you in the surefooted knowingness that you can and will overcome all. You will reap the gifts of challenge.

Be tenacious in all you say and do. Persist in your desires. Hold your Divine principles without compromise. Allow your Divinity within to be made manifest with tenacity. Your tenacity of spirit is revealed in the words you say and the deeds you do. Are you tenaciously Divine in all you say and all you do?

Remember that love requires tenacity. To love yourself requires tenacity. To love another requires tenacity. Your tenacity of spirit will sustain you when the world leaves you and the lover abandons you.

Tenacity of Spirit must be cultivated. Recall all the times in your life that you overcame the odds to be here today, that was your tenacity of spirit. Thus, you have a foundation on which to build your path ahead. Your labour will be worthy and your toil rewarded. Be tenacious always...

Tenacity of spirit lies within you. Call the beast out
for the good of Self and for the good of all.

∞ Courage ∞

Courage is more than a feeling or mere sentiment of the self. Courage does not imply sacrifice, in that you have the courage to commit some great deed that you might lay your life down for another. Courage is a virtue of the soul. Courage is a way of being. Courage is an act of faith...a faith in action. Courage is saved for the worthy moment; when you awaken to all that has been before in the yearning for a new way of being.

Courage is only required for the moment when you come face to face with yourself. You must call out your courage. Do not retreat from the sight of yourself in that given moment. You must have the courage to admit to yourself that all that has gone before in the presence of unknowingness was just so. And now the moment has arrived when you desire to live your life as an expression of the Divinity within. That moment, my friend is the only moment worthy of courage.

In your land and corner of the Earth, it is at times difficult to remain true to your Divinity; it is difficult to wake up in a world that prefers you asleep. For when you face yourself, others are compelled to face themselves. When you are courageous and live in tandem with your Divinity within, you are opposed to the one who desires to remain dormant to themselves. Yet, know that whilst rebuke may be present or put forth by another; know that you are presenting them with the opportunity to become themselves more fully and expansively. Maybe today that might not recognised as such but know that tomorrow you might be their inspiration.

It remains courageous to stand firm in the face of thyself. Face only yourself with courage, for it is you that must exist with you. You are answerable to yourself. You must understand that courage is never to be used in opposing another; we only ever oppose ourselves and resist our Divinity within. And in the moment when you know, you have opposed yourself, hold yourself in your courage. Thou art thine own provider, the safe keeper of thine soul, the king and labourer of thine land.

Choose to live your life from your Divinity within; choice will present itself in any given moment. Hold thine courage firm in thine hand, for you are capable of greatness and splendour in the arena of your soul. You are your attorney to Self, the judge and jury of thine own performance. Have courage and be courage. You must face yourself with an insatiable desire to unleash the Divinity within.

Courage is for the worthy moment. Face thyself.

14

∞ Humility ∞

Be humble of heart; a humility embraced with a conviction of the soul. Humility does not mean that you are shy or unworthy of all that has been bestowed to you. Rather, be humble in the knowledge that you are carved from the hand and heart of the Divine. You are a sculpture of the Divine...be humble in this knowledge alone.

Reminisce on the creation that is you. Allow the knowledge of your own magnificence to touch you deep within, to hold you solid in times of challenge and turbulence. Know with a sure humility that these changes will unmask the deep beauty within. You are and always will be a Divine gift; your purpose special, your potential unlimited and your presence meaningful. Rather, than remain on land, your soul is destined to fly.

Never shrink back from the challenge. Never hide the truth of who you are from another nor least of all from yourself. Be humble in your specialness for within you Divinity is found. Be humble before the Master who hath created you in his likeness and allow the gentle tears to fall from your eyes. Do not be incredulous to the masterpiece of you. Be humbly honoured that much arduous creative spiritual toil was placed into the invention that is you.

Remember, within you lies a treasure; a unique offering only you bring. Although the journey may be arduous, there is no doubt that the perfect potential of your purpose will surely guide you home. Inside, in the depths, you already know your gifts. The challenge arises when you must trust the path that will lead you to bestow your gifts to the world around.

Be humble in your treasure, yet surefooted in your sharing of your riches. How do I find my gifts? Simply find that space within and ask thyself the question, what is my potential? What is my purpose? Where does my joy lie? As you desired so you shall find.

Wait patiently for the answer, in full trust that the answer will come. Trust my child. And as your request is fulfilled, be humble in the knowledge that you are simply a vessel. You manifest your potential and purpose in the world, in honour of the Divine. Be humble in the incredulous voice within, which speaks softly with a loving compassion that says: 'who me? I never knew that such creative joy existed...that fulfilment satiated the soul...that I am a masterpiece and vessel of the Divine and it is my birth right to share my Divine gifts, that the Divine, I and the world might be honoured'.

You are a masterpiece and a vessel of the Divine.
Honour the Divinity within and above.

15

∞ Honour ∞

To honour is to hold sacred. Honour thyself; hold thyself sacred. Remember the Truth of what you are...a vessel of the Divine. Honour all that is you; your shining light, your heart, your soul, your thwarted aspects of the self; your flaws.

Pull gently on the threads that are your flaws. Allow them to unravel. Pull not with haste; softly and slowly for behind this protective curtain lies a precious entity; your vulnerability. She demands a gentle hand and a nurturing spirit. She the flaw that held the vulnerability demands to be honoured also.

Honour is a virtue; the life spring of your soul. Honour is your admittance and allowance to walk this land in honesty of all that thou art; Divine. Honour must be made visible in thy land and tribe. Honour is made known in your words and your deeds. Do your words and deeds manifest your honour?

Fear not the virtue of honour. For in being of honour, you call others to be of honour in their undertakings with you. Your honour is a gift gently wrapped in the truth of your soul. Your honour reveals you as trustworthy, surefooted, and solid.

Complete all your dealings in the spirit of honour. Speak not ill of another, for judgement of another will sequester your honour to a place of silence. Holding your honour in this prison, you will unwittingly imprison yourself. You will unintentionally rob another of the opportunity to manifest their honour in your presence.

Your word is pertinent, but your deeds must be in alignment with your word for your honour to be brought forth. Thy words and thy deeds from the Divinity within are to be held sacred; they are to be honoured.

Speak and act in accordance with the Divinity within. In this precious practice, you can rest peacefully with yourself. The honour that sends you forth in the world guiding your word and deeds is the same virtue that replenishes your spirit in the dark of the night.

Hold thyself, thy words, and thy deeds sacred. Move with honour and meet with honour. Be fearless in your honour. Freedom of thy Self and all who cross your path will be the ensuing gift.

To honour is to hold sacred...hold thyself sacred.

Michelle Stone

∞ Pain ∞

Pain is the prison and you are the prisoner. Whilst pain and suffering may be contended as a facet of the human condition, pain is a state that arises when one is unable to resolve and reconcile their experiences within. As one fails to resolve and reconcile their experiences within, one is unable to integrate their new learning. The painful state precedes the healing process and thus the painful state serves to contrast the healed state. As one knows pain and the healing process, then and only then can one become anew and know their wholeness within.

Pain gifts you the journey of healing. Healing is both a gentle process and a gentle master. Pain can be a harsh custodian. He walks the corridors of your prison. He ensures that another can never come close to enter and cause more pain; the custodian of your soul inadvertently imprisons you. Pain may have robbed you of intimacy and connection but you must know as she has taken so she shall return. Pain is your ally as she may have protected you when you were unable to protect yourself.

When you so desire, the custodian of your soul that is pain may become your ally. Pain being healing waiting to take place is your debtor with many dividends to repay you. Your reimbursement will be sweet albeit thy labour might be arduous. When you are ready and formidable to re-negotiate your contract with pain, your liberation and return to grace will begin.

Your endeavour with pain in the desire to return to the Divinity within bequeaths you a maturity of spirit. For once you know the depths of your own Self, then you can appreciate the depths of another. Pain gifts you compassion; in your battle with yourself, you must learn to gently hold yourself and in holding oneself one learns the beauty of holding another.

Pain protects the parts of you that are most vulnerable and most loving. The protector that is pain holds what is most precious and sacred in you. Pain is a protective parent and she will not allow what is most sacred and once harmed to be re-harmed. Only when you are ready will this protector step aside and trust you to take care of what is treasured. Whilst you may fumble at first in your journey as you learn to hold your vulnerability, with pace and ease you will learn to become a protective parent compassionately tending to your own wounds.

Pain bequeaths a maturity of spirit. The depths
of you are the depths of another.

∞ Faith ∞

Faith is the anchor of your soul. More rigorous than trust and more solid than knowing, she remains the steadfast holding in all of life's travesties. Faith is beyond mental abstraction or verbal expression. Faith emerges from action. For when you fly in faith once and the dividend revealed, you will be forever mystified by the seductress that is faith. She is a non-decisive, non-committal mistress. When you fly in faith, the destination or outcome is unknown. You are an unfolding story, each page and chapter yielding a dividend; an emerging scripture.

A scripture that is sacred, for to fly in faith is to allow the Divine, to be thine master and navigator. A union shared between you and the Divine. With an open hand and trusting heart, you unite with the Divine in a sacred trust that declares "take me where Thy will for Thou art my master. I succumb to You in the trust and honour that You will reveal to me all that I am destined to become, I am your subduing and willing slave, mystified that I am of You. You will hasten me to know only You".

Faith is a yielding endeavour. When you open your hand to the Divine and surrender, you experience a deep contentment in your soul. It is revealed to you that you need no longer push, nor toil aimlessly and tirelessly. In faith, you are held in the arms of peace and your spirit rests. Your heart trusts and your soul allows. Although you cannot see with your eye, your soul knows a deep certitude. Although you may be weary and confused, now you are a trusting child.

Faith known can never be unknown. Although she might be the seductive mistress, she is nonetheless an ever-present lover. For once you love her and know her, you will be forever entwined. After the initial seduction, you will be forever changed. Although you might protest and desire to be as you were before and try as you might to escape her charm, you will find yourself powerless.

You are powerless to evade and escape her love. Protesting to be thine own master and thine own determiner is futile; you must learn, in succumbing to faith, you become the gladiator of thine own soul. You are liberated.

> Faith is thine mistress and thou art the
> gladiator of thine own soul.

18

∞ Mercy ∞

You must learn to live in fellowship with your neighbours. You must strive to recognise yourself in your brother's eye. You are not separate; you are connected to all that is between you and all that is above you. Fellowship is developed through the practice of mercy. You are at the mercy of the Divine and you being of the Divine must learn the gift of mercy. The Divine has bestowed mercy to you, that you might bestow another.

Mercy demands spirit. She will break down all your barriers within. She will show where your weaknesses lie, where your bewilderment sleeps and where you are most determined to hold on to all that no longer serves you.

When you feel deeply affronted or pushed to the limit and the desire to condemn and condone is most strong and you are at the edge of declaring 'I can accept many things but this I cannot let go', in those moments mercy desires that you come to know her.

Mercy is not an immediate messenger. She is deliberate and discerning in her timing. She will only appear when you are ready. She will never be the unannounced or uninvited visitor. You, my child must invite her and grant her admittance into your heart. As she travels the land of your soul and gentle removes all that holds you back, you must patiently wait for her to complete her duty; you must forfeit to her.

Mercy means not that another might be saved the punishment of his crime. In saving another, you save yourself; mercy is your salvation. Mercy is the gift you give yourself because she allows the Divine within to re-emerge. The sins of another may cloak your soul, mercy will unveil the Divine within again.

The sins of another might block your light but mercy will re-ignite your spirit. Mercy will remove all that keeps you bound to another through deeds not of love, but rather deeds of fear and darkness. Mercy will remove the darkness of another, that speck nor stain will not dull all that is you.

Mercy is your salvation;
in saving another, you save yourself.

19

∞ Descent ∞

Do you remember your descent? Do you remember the times when you plunged into darkness? Descent is a feature of your existence; a facet of your experience. For you to know light, you must first wrestle with darkness. You must spend time in the dungeons of the self, battling the demons so that you will be free; free to be and free to see.

Fear not your descent, for in descending one must ascend. The depth of your descent determines the height of your ascension. So essentially the more you are willing to experience your darkness, the more simultaneously you will experience your light. In going down, you must come up. The depth of the down is the depth of the up.

I hear you ask, how do I handle my descent, if I go down I might never return? Never be afraid to know all that is within you. Remember darkness only exists to serve you in attaining your light. Fear not the ugliness, the pain, the disappointment, the wounded-ness, and messiness of your soul for these are the mere curators of your beauty. Do not despise them for they are senators of your treasure; they hold your beauty.

Since, they hold your treasure, they will not relinquish such prized objects willingly. Thus, you must battle with pain and his companions so that you might attain your due reward. Remember, although the battle might endure, you are of a relentless spirit.

There is no greater honour than to fight for the attainment of your own treasure.

Let the battle commence, let your soul guide you and the Divine hold you, as you descend and fight in honour of your Self and in honour of the Divine. You must fight to keep yourself in the arena. Never walking away, for to do so would dishonour all that is you. When you feel bruised and broken, your body aching and your soul shaking and the tiny voice whispers 'I give up, I desist', remember that is the moment in which you must hold on. Be relentless and steadfast and hear the roar of your soul, pushing you on.

Spirit will feed your hunger and wipe your brow. She will give you the final push to take you home. You simply must stay in the arena; for to leave is to leave you, to stay is to find, to fight is to gain, to descend empty is to ascend with treasure.

I descend and battle for all that is my Divine
inheritance; my birth right; my treasure.

20

∞ Reclaim Yourself ∞

Reclaim your destiny. Reclaim your Divinity; reclaim the Avatar within. You desired to know and all has been revealed to you in the words herein. Now you must journey forth, for once what thou hast sought has been revealed to you, it cannot be concealed. Everything revealed can never be concealed.

For as the soul within has been found, she can never be lost. Try as you might to escape the call of your soul in search of reprieve; what has been heard can never be unheard and the known can never be unknown.

Light does not vanquish darkness rather light dispels darkness. Darkness loses its power and steadfast hold in the presence of light. Light is a tender presence. She does not judge the darkness rather darkness is the obedient recipient of light's mercy. Light is the empress and in her presence, darkness is a willing servant. Darkness is humbled by her presence and nurtured by her acceptance of his presence.

Humbled, darkness will bow in gratitude. Darkness has been lonely, isolated, and vanquished. Light is the alchemist that facilitates darkness' return to beauty. Through their embrace, they find each other. Both darkness and light can only know their power and their limits when confronted with the presence of the other. Darkness and light reveal each other's strengths and potential. They liberate each other. Thus, each holds the key and power to the other's revelation, that they both might be known.

Thus, you must honour the shadows of thyself; the shadows of your soul. There is no brokenness, only beauty. There is no death only rebirth. There is no pain only knowledge and wisdom to be attained. There are no mistakes for the journey is infinite. The wrong turn preceded the right and thus all aspects of the journey brought you to this point today. To rebuke your past is to rebuke your present. To fragment your experience into good and bad would be to judge the traveller that is you.

Thus, you have made no wrong turns, no mistakes, and no wrongdoings; you are perfect.

As you reclaim yourself, your soul, the Avatar within,
may you do so in the full honour and gratitude for all
that was, in honour of all that is yet to be revealed.

21

∞ The Divine Embrace ∞

May I grant you mercy as I grant myself mercy. As I desire myself clean, may my radiant presence be a gift to you. May I commit myself to the path and journey ahead in the knowingness of the destiny woven in my soul. As I stand in the land of my reclaimed Self, may I honour all of me and all of you.

May I know that my hand lies in Your hand: The Divine and I are now one. Oh, that I might know that once my hand embraces Yours, I journey forth with an open heart and an open eye. I will never fall nor tumble, nor be lost, for in the Divine I am held. What is touched can never be untouched. Now I truly love You. I learned to love myself so that I might glimpse and share the eye of the Divine. I see myself through Your eyes and I know myself through Your heart. I know myself in Your sight and I can behold myself as You behold me.

I see what You see, I know what You know and from this day forth we are wedded as one. For as You proposed and asked for my hand, I willingly gave it to You.

Let the bells ring out, let the stars align, for now I am Divine. Destiny is my path and Source is my presence. I am in love. I am at one. I simply am...

I see what You see, I know what You know and
from this day forth we are wedded as one.

22

∞ Ambivalence ∞

Ambivalence is a sacred space of potential. In ambivalence, the desire for the new whispers softly, calling you forth that you might become an ever-present radiant light in the world. In ambivalence, you need not be afraid, you are simply ripe: simply ready for the new dawn. The mists of haze will part and a new journey will be revealed to you. Trust that thou art, right where, thou art destined to be.

The space of ambivalence might be likened to a space of suspension. You are ready to cast aside all that was in honour of all that is yet to come. As you cannot go back, you cannot go forward. You are suspended between the past and the future: between the lived and the yet to be revealed. Impatience may surround you as your desire to see your Self and your dreams manifest is fervent, but know my child, you must wait. Acknowledge the blazing fire in your beating heart that desires to propel you forward. Be at one with your heart and your desire. Be at one with yourself in the moment that is ambivalence.

Channel the energy of the space of ambivalence through the eyes of wonder. Turn your eye inward and speak to your soul; converse in reverential innocence. Ask her will I joyous in the space that is yet to come? Who will I be as I start anew? Am I yet all that I am destined to become? Who am I when I am separated from my past? Was my past, my foundations that I might be brought forth to become more Divine, more joyous, more present? Will all that I have left behind aid my seeking forth?

Listen in receptive wonder to the Divine within as she reveals all to you. Ambivalence calls you to connect with you; to be with you. In the space of potential and suspension you dwell. As you dwelt once, you will dwell again. As we journey forth with an unquenchable zest and insatiable desire to be more than we were than the moment before, ambivalence is the prized land between what was and what is destined to become.

Ambivalence is truly a sacred space bearing witness to the shedding of the past and the birthing of the new. Ambivalence is your holding space that you might be ready or the path ahead might be ready. The ambivalent state is necessary that you and the Divine might align, ambivalence mediates your timing with Divine timing. As the stars align for your path ahead, patience is prerequisite. Cosmic shifts of the Self and cosmic shifts of the universe need to fall into rhythm, that you might marry your beating heart with the rhythm of the Divine: That your tick might match the Divine tock.

Tick...tock...Tick...tock.

23

∞ The Spouse ∞

In all matters of the heart exercise discernment, but particularly, in deciding the one who is worthy of you. Yes, the one who is worthy of you!

You are firstly wedded to the Divine. As He has chosen you in full sight and delight of your magnificence, you must choose another in honour of the marriage you are already in. Once wedded to the Divine, you come to know your Divinity within and in this knowingness, the desire to compromise yourself is extinguished. Once you know your Self through the eyes of the Divine you will never compromise your Self or your Divinity within. As you are above so you are below.

Choose the spouse who is capable and worthy of holding all of you; all you are and all that you are destined to become. Choose the one who knows his own Divinity within. As he beholds his own Divinity within, he will behold yours. The loved is the beloved: as one is loved by the Divine only then is he capable of rising to become the beloved to another.

With such a spouse, you will never be wanting, for his own completeness will enrapture you and compel you to search out your own Divinity within. Thus, he will not give to you for he knows you do not lack. He knows that you do not need anything from within him. He is whole, you are whole. Thus, neither one needs from the other and now true love is possible.

The beloved is neither sought out nor yearned for. For in your marriage to the Divine you have surrendered to the power greater than yourself in absolute trust that He will reveal the spouse to you. As you reflect your wholeness to each other and attend to the knowingness within, you will know the spouse upon their arrival.

He will bring you forth and edify you in honour of the Divinity within and above. As you share the Divine with him, he will share the Divine with you. As the Divine knows you both, you will know each other. When your eyes meet the Divine within will softly whisper "I know you". As you journey forth the whispering of your soul will be "I know you as I know myself, you are my beloved and I am thine".

Let us honour the Divine as we honour each other. As the Divine, has revealed us to each other, our Divinity will surely be revealed to all. May this destiny take us to the perfect potential of all that we are and all that we are destined to become.

As one is beloved to the Divine only then is he capable
of rising to become the beloved to another.

24

∞ A Love Story Untold ∞

In the beating of your heart and the stirrings of your soul, lies the greatest love story yet untold. In the depths of you lies the lover within. A lover above all lovers. The lover that loves you in ways yet unknown. He will love you in ways unimagined. He will seek you out in ways unlike all his predecessors; he is the lover above all lovers.

This lover will never abandon you for he is steadfast in his holding, relentless in his desire, tenacious in his commitment and determination to know, love and honour all that is you. He is the bonafide warrior, the destiny maker, co-creator, truth seeker, peace pursuer, hate hater and eternal love maker.

Oh, that I would never shun the depths of my Self. Rather that I would become the greatest lover. The one who will tempt me to become all that I am destined to be. The greatest lover is I and the worthy recipient of my love is I. I lay myself bare before my Self. I explore myself in the presence of my own soul. I bring ecstasy to my Self. I make love to and through my own soul. I am the greatest lover and the greatest love story untold.

That I may become tender and turbulent in my love making as I unveil all that is I to the beloved that is I. And thus, may I practice love making with my Self so that I can truly make love to another. May I hear the call of my own soul before I hear the call of another. May I edify and sanctify my own soul. May I make love in ways untold and unknown to my Self. Thus, in the arms of another, I am only held by the moment preceding wherein I held my Self.

Within me lies the greatest love story, a story untold waiting to unfold. I am the greatest lover and the worthy recipient of love. I am the uncontested lover and worthy recipient of my own love. I am the beloved at one with my Self and the Divine. Thus, I may become: the adorer and the adored, the beholder and the beheld, the warrior and the surrendered, the devoted and the devotee, the inspirer and the inspired, the giver and the receiver, the complete and the undiscovered, the perfect and the imperfect. And in my stance and in my becoming, I am whole. Thus, I come before you not in search, rather in the truest spirit of sharing, that you and I might find exuberance in the other's completeness and unity within. Thus, as you and I are unified within, may the Divine delight and behold all that is you and all that is I and all that is us.

The greatest lover is I and the worthy recipient of my love is I.

∞ Authenticity ∞

May you always know who you are in the moment herein. May you come to know your own authenticity. Be cautious in your self-definition, for as you say you are, thus you become. You do not need to know, who you were in the week past nor the week forth, it is only desirable that you know who are in the moment that is.

You do not need to know all things nor all understandings, it is more pertinent that you know your stance in the moment that is now. In this manner of self-definition, you remain open to your unfolding and evolving self. Thus, who you are today may not be who you will be tomorrow. You are in the dynamic flux of your own evolution. You are not prisoner to your self-definition rather you are a liberated soul full of both the known and the unknown.

You are always a masterpiece in the making, an incomplete painting, an unending story, and an infinite song. What has gone before is mere testament of all that is yet to come. As you travel ahead, experience teaches you. You are an ever-present and willing learner. You desire to know all the you that is you and all the I that is I. As you conquer your experience and the challenge set forth, you are both the student and the master.

As life touches your spirit and teaches your soul, may you come to know your desire to learn is always nourished. And thus, your potential is infinite. May you come to only know who you are in the moment that is. In this way of knowing you are aligned with authenticity and in being true to who you are, you grant another the potential to be true to you. As you honour all of who you are, you are surefooted in the knowingness that another must surely be true to his Self. Thus, your authenticity ignites the perfect potential of the space that lies between you.

May your authenticity, liberate you and liberate another. May you be true to your heart's desires. As your soul calls you forth may you honour the call and respond. May you move with swiftness if your soul so desires. May you sit in stillness if your soul so desires. May you thus be accountable to your Self and to the truth and trust of who you are, in honour of all that is. May you be confident in your desire to reveal your Self to yourself and to another. For in another you see your Self and in you he sees his Self. Accordingly, you bear witness to your Self so that another might witness and know all that is you and of you.

What is desirable is that you know who
are you in the moment that is.

26

∞ Connection ∞

May you and I connect with each other. May we find our common ground and shared destiny. For as I have travelled so too have you travelled. In our moments of sharing, may we recognise each other in the tales that are recanted and retold with fondness of who I and you were: travellers on the path. And although our paths might not have been identical, they are essentially similar. For in this moment as we stand before each other, we have met and connected with each other in each other.

May you connect with your Self in all things. Then you have the potential to connect with another. As you find all that lies within, you will reclaim your connection to the Divine also. I connect with my Self, you connect with your Self. Thus, we share a connection reflective of the other. A connection designed by the Divine, for it is He who has placed you on my path and as you were placed, I have so found. As guided I followed and thus a new moment was found.

May you know the capacity of every encounter; a potential connection. For as the experience has been good or bad, desired or resisted, irrespective you connected. You brought all of you to the moment and he brought all of him. The encounter brief or extended, nonetheless the connection occurred. For though at times as your mind idly wanders over the landscape of the past may you see all connections, in the moments that were as they were: travellers on crossed paths. Although your connection with another may have fed you or harmed you, nonetheless it taught you.

May you know when the moment comes when acting on the connection no longer serves both parties. May you have comfort in your parting in the knowledge that connections occur, end, reoccur and sometimes dissolve depending on the learning that is required or desired. May you never fear the connection with your Self. May you never fear connection with another. Connections serve a purpose of reinforcement of who you know your Self to be or expressive extension of all that you are and destined to become.

May connections be shaped by and in love and light. As you connect to the Divine, may another connect with the Divine within you. Accordingly, another will only be replenished and never depleted by your presence. As the Divine so desired that your paths might cross, you are here and he is here. May your connection below reflect the Divine above. You are you and another is you. Your story is another's story and all stories arise from the story authored and orchestrated by the Divine. Thus, you are connected.

May you know the potential for every encounter:
An Avatar connection in the making.

27

∞ The Desiring Spirit ∞

Oh, that you might never lose your hunger and thirst for the incoming experience. That you might never lay down and believe that you are satisfied and fulfilled, for there is always another moment to be savoured, another unknown to become known, a dream waiting to become a reality, a moment calling to be made a recollection.

The desiring spirit will move you forward in all things always and keep you striving to become all that you might be in each moment. In the absence of the desiring spirit one is already deceased: beaten down by life. Thus, in the pivotal moment you must allow your desiring spirit to emerge. There is no settling or compromising. You are never done rather always becoming. This is the way of the warrior within.

The desiring spirit moves you to become all that you are destined to become, feeding your potential and triumph in equal measure. Potential and triumph are proportionate partners and the desiring spirit bequeaths both in equal measure.

Know that the tasks set before you, are never more than you can accomplish. Mastery is always assured for the Divine solely seeks that you conquer and become. The challenges set forth may vary in what they call forth in you. The Divine desires for the champion within you to be revealed and revelled in all tasks, challenges, and ways.

The desiring spirit meets the experience and in meeting the

experience, your inner landscape is revealed to you. You come to know your strength, your compassion, and the limits to your love. You make known your honour, your wisdom, your truth, your unlimited potential, and infinite greatness; for this you are and this you are destined to become.

Desire the dream and dare to live the dream. Set aside all limiting beliefs, reason, and rationality; the mere abstractions of your mind. See the dream, live the dream and be the dream. Align with the Divine for similarly and reassuringly the Divine desires that you might become all that you are destined to become. Once you desire this for yourself, you are always supported and powerfully protected. All obstacles fall away and you both know the destination. You must only walk the path.

Trust the path, trust the process, trust you always.

∞ Momentum ∞

Momentum comes in many forms: from within, from above and from another. At times, you may effortlessly propel yourself forward. The Divine flame within blowing vigorously and you are relentless in your pursuit. Nonetheless, at other moments it may be the love and belief of another in your venture that will carry you when your feet wane or perhaps pain overcomes you...

Ever-present, available, and accessible is the love and belief of the Divine. This momentum will carry you forth and set you apart. When your own momentum wanes, may you have another to call upon and may the Divine within your ally re-ignite the Divine within you; may the Divine above make His presence known.

When the task is challenging, may you be focused, relentless, single-minded, and single-eyed with the Divine. Thus, all necessary momentum is abundantly available. If you need a gentle breeze or a chariot of force, the sought will be known and the desired for obtained.

Impel and compel yourself forward always in all things. When you fall, may the Divine of another or the Divine above catch you and gently release you on your path again. May you know, both the gentleness and relentlessness of this momentum and the moment that matches both. Channel your momentum wisely: tapered or unleashed. May you deliberately discern the moment and the momentum necessitated.

Michelle Stone

As the moment requires, may the momentum come from within, above or another. May you move in tandem with the moment that is, in the assurance and trust that all is well and all required is supplied. May you come to know the beauty and mercy of momentum. In times when you move forward in haste and aimlessness, may momentum decrease for the speed of the soul is beyond the speed of the mind. When the soul moves with a gentle surefooted motion, may the momentum of the mind not squander the momentum of your soul.

Trust you must; trust the momentum of your soul above the momentum of your mind. As the mind, may take you to places unknown, unyielding, undesired, and unrequired, remember that these destinations are illusions and simply a form of avoidance of the moment that is. The soul will also take you to destinations unknown and these places are the terrain of tomorrow: real, authentic, and true. This envisioned ground is the land in which you are sure to arrive, see and come to know. Rather than figments of a fractured mind they are real places on your path ahead.

May you deliberately discern the moment
and the required momentum.

29

∞ The Visionary within ∞

Hold a vision in all things, remaining mindful of the ego's desire to control your experience. In seeking to control your experiences you inadvertently control the experience of another also. By extension you control the perfect potential of the space between you. As you limit yourself, you limit another and you both limit the potential of the moment therein.

Rather than seeking to control the moment, the visionary within knows, in every moment the vision is only to act in accordance with Divine principles. The guiding foremost principle being, in every experience you bring the best of you.

Vision is a prerequisite for manifestation. In knowing the Divine that you desire, you hold a vision and this vision sustains you. You hold firm and true, believing in perfect possibility and perfect potential. You move forward guided by your aspiration. The visionary within is powerful.

Hold a vision within you for every encounter. The vision being to bring forth all of you, the best of you to share with another. In doing so, may you both share the best of who you are and the best of the moment therein. In holding a vision for the moment, you must also hold a vision for your being: finite and infinite. Throughout your time on the earth in which you dwell may you find your vision for life and may destiny guide you to your life's potential and purpose.

May your vision and desire, reveal to you what you are destined

Michelle Stone

to bring and destined to be. Like a skilful carpenter may you know that every required tool lies within you to create your life, your path, and your revelation. You are a tradesman and your unique skill and craft is your trade. Shedding, paring, sanding, perfection is a process of patience. The revelation of beauty is not time bound. One will only know beauty once revealed.

The true carpenter whilst holding a vision will know perfection, only when he looks at the product of his labour. The vision attained, the soul will be content. You know neither through the eye nor mind but rather through the soul's sensation to what the eye discloses.

Hold a vision in all things, remaining mindful of
the ego's desire to control your experience.

30

∞ The Gifted Opportunity ∞

The gifted opportunity as so she suggests is the opportunity not sought, rather the opportunity that you stumble or fall into and if one can be self-honest and declare- "I know neither why I am here nor why this is happening, yet I trust, yet I trust, yet I trust". Then one will come to know the gifts of the opportunity, as one allows one's Self to live out the experience in trust. Thus, in trusting the experience, one aligns oneself with the opportunity to be gifted. Rewards will be found, a beauty discovered, a treasure revealed. Trust in your investment and trust in your return.

Return may be in many forms: learning of oneself or life, a virtue within reclaimed, self-understanding that aids understanding of another, the shedding of an illusion or the revelation of a truth. Whatever the form, when you stake your trust in the experience, your dividend is assured. No trust, no bond equals no reward. Although, you may be hesitant or reluctant to stake your name, destiny is calling you forth to engage with the experience. If you align your name as destiny calls, you are in sync, in flux and in flow; you are the Divine drifter.

It remains simple that the experience and opportunity is here, pleasing or displeasing to your sight, resistance is fearful and futile. You cannot go back. You can only move forward. So, move forward with trust that the experience desired or not is here and as the experience has shown up, so too must you show up. To accept or decline the experience is sometimes out of your hold.

Michelle Stone

Thus, it remains that you have the choice to trust that this is the gifted opportunity that happened before and will happen again. You have the power to reap a reward if you so desire. You might become a wealthy master from the experiences you have not sought, yet not resisted.

And as you place your hand in the Divine, trusting in all that is, as a trusting child your hand rests open. Thus, your hand being open, you are ready to receive. To receive your gift, you may have to walk with blind faith. Remember you need not your eye to receive now. Solely, you need an undefended heart and hand. The Divine will place the reward or return for your trust in His plan for you in your vulnerable hand.

You engaged with the experience and resisted not what was. Thus, you are an investor in the plan, in the process and in the return. As the Divine, has invested in you, you invest in Him and you are partners in the plan, in the process and in the return.

You might become a wealthy master from the experiences you have not sought, yet not resisted.

31

∞ Common Ground ∞

Oh, that you would come to know the meadow that is common ground. The land where you and another are one with the One. Unified in your desire for the same, for the good of each other, another or for all. A land where you align with another for a moment, for a while, for a space in time. 'Tis a miracle that you and another found each other in this space in this place.

In this space and place, you could come to know each other in part. You desire the same for a moment in time. Your destiny shared and a glimpse of the Divine is revealed. For in another you see you and in you, he sees himself. In the great story that is your unfolding destiny, your encounter with another a paragraph, a page, a chapter or perhaps the fullest of stories. For a moment in time you were not alone, fumbling in isolation. You were briefly on common ground with another. Their presence affirming, their sharings familiar and the weary traveller you may have been, is now both the companion and the accompanied.

Their company on the path brought you hope and light. Their desire to continue and to strive at times carried you and you would like to know that you carried them. 'Twas an effortless honour, as you carried each other. Both were edified and exalted and in that moment, it all made sense for the Divine brought you to another and another to you. You were never alone for the Divine was with you both and orchestrated your encounter. Thus, where two were on common ground there now stands three.

Michelle Stone

And thus, their presence on your path in the land of common ground brought you shelter and a will to continue. You knew that your desires were to be found in another and their desires to be found within you. And thus, you learned that whilst you may doubt yourself and your path and the desires of your heart… in the land of common ground solace will be found. Whilst you know that another cannot travel for you nor you for another, you remained grateful for the presence of another on your path. Surely, as you both may have been lost before, now you point the way for each other. You trust all that was before this space, in the trust of all that may emerge from whence you leave this place.

Surely 'tis so, that as the Divine enshrines your journey apart and together, the land of common ground will be found. When what is within aligns with what is without and all align with what is above.

> As two shooting stars, may cross on a path, the point
> of intersection is the brightest point, for in this point
> two align with the light above, in common ground.

32

∞ Reconciliation ∞

Forgiveness appears to be the commonly employed term to describe the process or outcome wherein one attempts to let go or overcome the trials and tribulations of this life or experience and thus I tell you truly that perhaps more than applying the term of forgiveness you might employ the term, reconciliation. Forgiveness can be misunderstood to imply superiority. One must give for another to receive...the innocent and the convicted, the perpetrator and the victim.

Reconciliation a far more apt term, describes a process and or outcome that at times can be achieved by both parties simultaneously or a journey that both must pursue independent of each other. Firstly, you must reconcile the experience with you within you. You must come to your own understanding of your own hurt or betrayal or whatever the correct description of your experience. You must journey within with yourself. You seek yourself out and if appropriate when you and the other have completed your inner reconciliation, you may complete your outer reconciliation together. Sometimes an outer reconciliation, whereby, one meets to exchange their experience of another with another is not desired and thus you must reconcile yourself with this understanding.

Thus, inner reconciliation does not always precede outer reconciliation. Accordingly, you may only reconcile your experiences within yourself. If you can complete this inner journey,

Michelle Stone

you can truly part company with another and move on with life or experiences as so desired. Thus, moving on at times truly means moving within.

Your story shared within another's story for now is complete. You have reconciled yourself with your Self and a new harmony discovered. A new strength reclaimed, for you can complete your story independent of another and another independent of you. Your unfolding story will be not be blighted or distorted by your time with another. You need not from another. You need only to reconcile yourself with your Self. Thus, you are free and another is free, both are in their truest states. Rather than being held captive by your stint with another, you are captivated by your own strength within. As you dissolved barriers within yourself, true beauty was found. Thus, you have not known yourself as you know your Self now.

Reconciliation describes a process and or outcome that at times can be achieved by both parties simultaneously or a journey that both must pursue independent of each other.

33

∞ Listening ∞

Can you hear me calling to you to come home to me and sit with me, to be with me for a while? I call you from within you. Though I am within you, closer than the call of another, at times you do not respond. You do not respond to you. You decline the invitation to be you with you. In this moment, you reject you and in another moment, you will hear you. The call of the Self is incessant and unrelenting; it is true to you.

Thus, to truly listen to another you must initially be present to all that is occurring within you. You must first hear your own story, to truly understand the story of another. If you can hear the depths within your Self, then surely you will come to know the depths within another. And thus, I ask you "can you be a gentle listener, listening to you? Can you strive to listen to you and rather than interpret or analyse your experience, can you simply listen to what it tells you, seeking only to observe and integrate it? Can you abstain from being your own critic and being a disinterested observer and simply be the present artist who illustrates or writes their picture or story within?"

Oh, how I longed for you to come home to you and hear me, that I that is thee, the protagonist in your own story. Rather than acting, you are real, rather than a prop you are solid. You show up for your own show before you show up for another. You see your Self before you see another. You seek within and thus you seek without. You know your own words. You know the lines within for you have listened diligently and acceptingly to yourself. You feel yourself within your ever-unfolding story and now you know where you have been, including the depths of you within you. Whilst at times a falling star, a villain, a victim, or a prop to another, now you know that as one falls one will surely rise again. Your tales are truly heard, tales of triumph, tales of challenge, tales of love and so you have known and so you are destined to become.

And thus, you have listened to you and thus you may listen to another. Now, may you both find each other in stories anew. For though your soul has revealed all to you, you know there is much more to come and much more to know. You have never known yourself like this in this moment that is. And thus, may you remember the powerful act that is listening. For in listening to yourself, you understand and come to know yourself, so that you might come to know you in your perfect form in all aspects of you. And may your listening grant you the gift of understanding and thus, in a moment you were not lost but found and held in the stories told and all those yet to unfold.

May you remember the powerful act that is listening
and find the depths within yourself and another.

34

∞ Unlimited ∞

There are no limits to where you have been and to where you might go. There are no limits to your story for it is unfolding. The song within has no ending, the journey has no destination, for you write on the page that is in your story within the scared scripture that is your life. Each day you begin anew. You travel only for the journey and desire of the destination. You move swiftly and with grace, held by the Almighty who leads you where you need to go, to who you are destined to be. You are unlimited and as you are unlimited, another is unlimited.

There are no limits to the potential within you. There are no limits to the potential within another and thus there are no limits to the potential of the space between you. There are no limits to the supply and nourishment from the Divine. If you searched the sky, you won't find any barrier or border. Thus, you fly freely for the beauty of flight anchored in the knowing that your resources are unlimited for a flight plan undefined that is sure to reveal what you need to know or where you need to be.

Limits are of the mind, for perhaps if you knew how free you are, the magic would only be momentary and thus your limitlessness is continually revealed and magic embraces you every day. And in this way, you receive an endless supply of enchantment and surprise and accordingly your joy is limitless and continually experienced.

As your story unfolds you are reminded of how unlimited you are. There are no limits to where you have been and there are no limits to where you might go. If you could truly remember the unfoldment that is you, then surely you would come to know that the most beautiful piece of art is the picture that is incomplete. The story that is truly treasured is the one that captivates you, a complete yet incomplete mystery. And thus, as you know and accept that it is the unknown that draws you forward and as you know you can truly never fully know, you are compelled to live, engage, and explore the moment that is in the full knowledge, desire and surety of the unknown moment that is yet to become.

The only way to travel is with a surety of the prize to be found that embraces uncertainty. In the knowledge that whilst this moment may be complete it only serves to reveal and lay foundation to the moment that is yet to come. For moments are unlimited that you too might come to know your Self as infinite...

Limits are of the mind. The soul is infinite.

35

∞ The Craft and the Crafted ∞

That you might come to know that within lies both the master and the masterpiece. You have an unlimited potential and the meticulous skill to create your path. You carve the wood of your soul, sharpening, and shredding all that is not you and all that is not of you to reveal an unmatched, un-contended masterpiece.

As you have been created by the Divine, engineered to endure, perfectly designed, you are the treasure and the treasured. Oh, that you might know that the master crafter lies within you, whose task remains to remove all falsehood, all sense of ever being misguided and being average or standard, replicated or duplicated. For you are an original authentic presence never to be repeated.

And thus, with this in mind and with that in heart, you must take your tool bag and commence the craft for which you are inherently calibrated for and craft for you by you. Thus, you are the craft and the crafted.

Toil gently and diligently for a masterpiece is both a delicate process and product. You are commissioned to create and all requirements are supplied. Labour patiently, yet painstakingly. May you relish in the process and the product; the craft and the crafted.

And when the moment of reveal is nigh, embrace the gasp and sighs of your adoring audience. Who with a hand on heart shall declare "In you I see beauty and so, as my hand is delicately placed upon my own heart I shall use the same hand to craft my own masterpiece for as the hand of the Divine is indiscriminate in touch…so too shall I become the master and the masterpiece".

You are the master and the masterpiece. You are the craft and the crafted. You are truly Divine.

36

∞ Your Word ∞

Your word is your virtue, your honour, your integrity...your truth. Your word is your promise as you reveal yourself to another. Your word is of your soul, a wellspring of purity flowing forth that you might allow another to know you. Your words are partly responsible for the beauty of the space between you and another.

May you choose your words with due diligence and discernment in honour of the power implicit in your words. Your words reveal you to the world. Thus, you may show your Self as the wise and powerful empress that lies within you. Your words may lift another or slay the spirit of another. Thus, may you only choose and use words in cognisance and passionate awareness of the vulnerability of another. Thus, may the words of you that are found in another, be only the words that nourish and nurture the delicacy of their being.

Your word is of you. Thus, may you behold the power and potential of your word to reveal you. You show yourself in your word to the world of another. Sit with thy Self and like an eager student allow your words to come from the deepest space that lies within you...for this is the word you can trust. It is the word upon which you can build yourself and thrust yourself forth. For the word that is found within, is one of promise and potential, the most reliable and trustworthy compass and truth detector. Your word tells another who you are and the fullness of trust that lies within you.

Thus, may you never abuse the power and potential of your word by speaking ill of another, by taking their character unjustly, or touch their soul in a harsh and harmful manner. You are of the Divine and thus may your word be only of the Divine. In honouring our word, we honour the space of Divinity that lies within and between us.

Take your words seriously. Give sober ponder to the utterances of your mouth and the space from which they come forth. Try to ensure that your words are of your soul and not of some wounded space that lies within you. Choose and trust your words, rather than taking the words of another. Learn to express yourself with words that are expansive and of depth. These words lie within you and thus you must find the word to reveal the You within you.

Your word is your virtue, your honour,
your integrity...your truth.

∞ Your Tribe ∞

Who are your tribe, your people, your allies, your companions, and your true group? You choose them and they choose you in resonance and accordance of what lies within you and all that lies within them. They crossed your path and this was destined to be so. When they crossed your path, they were destined to stay with you for a while or a lifetime. For in another, you knew a solid companion was to be found, one that would walk with you or carry you forth when your own soul was weary from the waves of this lifetime. As you choose your tribe, another too must choose their tribe.

Listen to what lies within you and to what lies within another. Is this other of due diligence and decency, an honourable other, a loyal and trustworthy companion? In asking this of another, you must also ask this of yourself. What mark of a man is this? What mark of a man are you? For in choosing the tribe you too must be of the tribe.

When the moment of risk is around or your battle is nigh, call on your tribe, be assured that they will come and be found at your back, at your side, or marching protectively ahead of you. When the abyss threatens your path and you are too weary to jump or devise some creative strategy to navigate the giant hole, you are in danger of falling into...your tribe will lie down and join their bodies that they might form a bridge on which you can walk and thus they are of strength with an unbreakable back. The tribe

Michelle Stone

together is a mighty force and a treasure chest of creativity, for in one or many, a creative strategy or solution to your predicament is to be found.

Whilst you choose your tribe, you know that the Divine enshrines every experience. He places the warrior within and the warrior on the path. You recognise the warrior in your Self then surely it is so that you will be able to know the warrior within another. Be of good measure and be of great intention. And whilst the power of the tribe lies within you, you can meld your potential with the potentials of others. For conjoined forces are of conjoined potential and sealed with Divine intent, victory for you and your tribe are thus assured. Me + you + Divine = certitude.

What mark of a man are you? For in choosing
the tribe you too must be of the tribe.

38

∞ Stable & Solid ∞

You are stable and solid; stable in the hand of the Divine and solid in the Divine that lies within you. You are of self-certitude and solid in the path you thus walk. You are held solid, by the deepest space within. You are stable in the thread that holds you from above, stable enough to move gently, yet strong enough to be anchored from above when your feet are apart from the ground upon which you desire to walk.

May you touch and firmly hold the Divinity within. When held tightly and fearlessly, you are solid. You can trust yourself and thus you are trustworthy to another. Your loyalty to yourself is found in your loyalty to another. Your integrity within strengthens the bonds of both your words and relationships. You are surefooted and trusting, for the path is of the deepest part of you and the deepest part of you is most steadfast and true. You are simply being You and in this state of simplicity, you are solid.

The Divine above holds you firmly and flexibly. The thread is unbreakable. You are moving forth with stability. As the waves of life move you, your anchor above will rise you up or drop you deep below to dodge or submerge you as the Divine so desires, until the sea is gentle and calm again, that you might sail effortlessly forth. Whilst the anchor from above may not be required in the calm sea, it is always a consoling presence. For if this stable anchor was removed or you were remiss of its' presence, fear and haste would cause you to topple your raft, to believe that you were lost with no certitude of being found, rescued, or restored again.

Thus, you are of a stable anchor and of a solid space, destined to roam, sail and fly without assurance of any place. Companions will be many, for your solid presence promises them a strong holding space should they ever need shelter from the seas of life. Solid in Self and stable from above, you are an adventurous traveller taking risks and blazing trails. Both the Divine above and within guides your path and sets you free. A bold adventurer lies within you, waiting to be found, longing to discover new places and spaces that will feed your daring heart...

The thread between the Divine within and
above is unbreakable: stable and solid.

39

∞ Gratitude ∞

Give thanks and receive grace in all things, places, and spaces. Never feel or believe that any moment is incomplete nor any desire yet unfulfilled. Seek and find solace in the full knowledge and knowingness that there is never anything lacking or missing. Everything is just so and just so is…enough.

If one falls into the snare of believing that there is something missing in this great moment that is, then you merely are the missing one. For one does not see, that all in the moment therein is enough and all as all…is destined to be so.

Gratitude is and will remain the currency of continuation. If you can buy into the moment that is, due reward will thus be returned to you and thus if you can do, another can do. Be just so, and if you give of your gratitude to all the moments and lands wherein you find yourself, then you will be a wise investor, investing freely and completely in the moment that is. This investment will yield a due bounty to you.

For as you invest of your gratitude, return is assured and your return will be sweet. Gratitude in all things, places and spaces may not initially be effortless. You may need to be a reluctant investor. Nonetheless, reluctant, or willing the investment is made and thus as you must, you will yield.

Gratitude may support you in simplifying your journey as preceding gratitude your required state is acceptance. Once you walk in acceptance, reluctant or free, you are always in sync and in flow with what is rather than what is not. Thus, the path whilst bumpy is smooth, whilst unknown is also known. You can trust that thou art exactly where thou art fated to be and all is as all is designed to be. You are at one with the moment and the moment at one with you. All that remains, is for you to give thanks for all that was, is and yet to be known.

Gratitude is the way of the gracious traveller.

40

∞ The Leader within ∞

Who is the ruler of your kingdom? Who sets the codes whereby you live your life? Who governs your soul? Who dictates your opportunities? Who declares the freedom of your soul? Who reigns in the landscape of your inner terrain? Who says where you might roam? Who is the guardian of your home? Who is the gatekeeper of your path and of your light? Who is your protector and leader? To whom do you pledge your worthy allegiance?

Surely, you must know that you always commence with thyself, prior to pledging with another and thereby within you the leader lies.

You are a leader above all others. Within your life, you dictate to and with yourself. You have the potential to make wise judgements and to issue wise decrees. You have the potential to inspire others, to create your following, to walk behind your name...you are a leader.

You are the leader, just and true who governs your soul. All desire to greet you, see you and come to know you. You raise yourself up, write your own story and resolve conflict within and without. You are a leader.

The seed of a leader lies within you and as you nourish this seed so too will others, for in you they will see the man in the making, the king in the becoming, the leader above all others emerging. As you inspire, so too will others be inspired and thus, you and they both become the inspiration longed for by another. You are the path lighter, destiny maker, gracious taker, free giver, soul creator.

You must own your own seed and nurture same said seed forth. It will rise from the ground to become a temple of magnificence, a tower of strength, solid and steadfast. You trust in you and the call you make....

You lead your story, your becoming, your potential, and your truth. As you stake your name and stake your faith with the seal of the Divine, a pact strong and true will bring pure justice to you and all who follow the leader who lies within you.

Within you the leader above all leaders lies.

41

∞ Bringing it ∞

You are bringing it, the best of you to every given moment wherein you find yourself. You are bringing it to each encounter you find yourself in with another. To every single role or any title, you find your name pledged under, you are bringing it.

In every moment, you find yourself, know the wellspring that lies within. Inside you, lies all that you might ever need. You are equipped with every tool, virtue, and solution that you might ever require. You are never in want or lack, for as the moment calls you forth, you can deliver! As is required you can bequeath. You are bringing it and bringing it you are deemed to do so.

So, that you might bring it, you must first know the landscape within you. You must know the architecture of your soul: the Divine above and the Divine below. As you know, you can bring and bequeath.

When the moment calls and much is required, know that within you lies courage to behold, courage immeasurable, a lion's heart with a mighty resounding roar. Everyone will see and come to know, you are bringing it. You are showing up powerfully in all you say and do. Power lies within you. A power that is infinite. You show up powerfully and bring it; every creative solution, the deepest virtue, the kindest heart, a relentless and redemptive mercy. You are bringing it, in honour of all that lies in waiting within you and in the fullest honour of all of you. You bring it, that you might be known, seen, and revealed for the magnificence that thou art; the one of the One; the greatest one.

You are bringing it and another is bringing it. Thus, may you offer it up, in honour of all that lies within and above. Embrace every given moment and every given encounter in the solid knowledge that you are bringing it. And as you bring it, so too shall another be compelled to bring it. Thus, you create a space of beauty, potential and truth between you.

Know you and bring you. Liberate you and may your liberation inspire another. Thus, you no longer need to control, distort, or manipulate the moment or another. You know that you are bringing it. And as you bring, you shall truly receive as the hand of the Divine works through and around you. The most natural within and around you unfolds. Thus, you know you are in a truly sacred land: the unfolding moment.

When the moment calls and much is required, know that
within you lies courage to behold, courage immeasurable,
a lion's heart with a mighty resounding roar.

42

∞ The Leap of Faith ∞

You have called and expectantly desired that your moment might come. Now the beautiful moment is no longer hidden and thus revealed and a leap of faith is required. You must leap into the unknown and learn the gift of blind faith. When your moment is of the leap of faith, know that you are calibrated to fly and dazzle all who look upon you. You leap, you fly.

There is no more required than being who thou art. For within, you are calibrated for courage, meticulously designed, skilfully and tenderly designed to fly. And thus, rather than leap you must fly with blind faith and a reliable compass. There is no place to travel only into the moment that is. The leap of faith is calling you and as she calls you must answer.

Thus, be courageous in your flight as you journey from the land known to a destiny unknown. You will learn the power of belief that you hold within and around you. In the moment, you will soar with momentum unknown. You will be fully alive as thou art destined to be. As you fly, you will come to know that thou are always protected and divinely guided. Thus, in this steadfast knowledge you will be content of a beautiful joy as your soul smiles; a smile of mystery and of knowingness. The voice within sweetly declares "now I know that I am the greatest and never alone, for as the Divine within has brought me here, the Divine will surely guide me home".

Thus, that you might know, within you lies the insatiable desire

Michelle Stone

for the moment of your leap of faith. You desire the breakdown of your imagined barriers within and the removal of the pretence of your existence. You desire to know and affirm yourself of infinite potential and power. As so desired, you will come to know, that faith is flight and flight is faith. You are of the sky and destined to fly.

Seek and you will find the moment above
all moments: the leap of faith.

43

∞ The Tale within a Tale ∞

The Divine has created a tale within a tale. A tale lies within the yearnings of your heart. In the tale of all that is…lies your tale. Your own story is within the greater story. Thou art a story in yourself, connected to the larger story of all that is.

As your tale of greatness unfolds, so too does the tale of all that is. Your tale is connected to the tale of another and both are connected to the tale of the Divine. As the Divine, has authored the story of greatness of all that is, so too a spectacular tale is etched in your soul. Thou art calibrated to unleash a tale of magnificence to all around you.

Ponder the vastness of the creativity of the Divine, who has created a story for each and a story for all. Further the Divine has created a story for the evolution and betterment of the collective. What tale of magnificence lies within you? The sharing of your story may ignite the story of another; a tale of one, is a tale of all.

You are a tale within a tale, a book within a collection, a verse within a universal song and a melody within a harmony. You are a story within a story.

Thus, may you come to know the story that lies within you. Great suspense surrounds you. Where have you been? Where are you destined to go? What have you come to know? What have you yet to learn? You are a thriller within a thriller, a mystery within a mystery, a romance within a romance, a reference within a reference. As the Divine is author to all and the Divine lies within you, thus thou art an author.

Write your own story well. May it be enshrined with truth and light. May your story be a beautiful unveiling of you as you write to find and become. Take the pen of the Divine within your hand and within your heart. Write from your soul, for therein lies a story yet to be told.

> You are a tale within a tale. You are a story
> within the greater story of all that is.

44

∞ The Architecture of Your Soul ∞

Within you lies a temple of magnificence; a delicately crafted temple. Whilst delicately created, it remains the strongest, most powerful fortress. That one might come to see and know the chambers of this temple; the spaces of strength, the spaces of honour, the spaces of integrity, the spaces of truth, the spaces of love. Spaces of solace and solitude, the spaces of wonder and enchantment, the spaces of solidarity within you.

A Divine premises is the architecture of your soul. A property of potential and promise, desirable and highly sought, reserved for you to view when thou shall desire. You have sought a place of wonder many a moment. I impart to you truly, the space of wonder that you seek lies within the space of wonder within you.

Build the temple of your soul on the word of truth. No stronger a foundation will ever be found. Should you ever believe or deceive yourself that another foundation is desirable then I tell you your tower and temple shall surely crumble. All that is not of the Divine is temporary, fleeting and wholly unreliable.

The architecture of your soul will not sit upon such foundations. The plan does not match the place. Thus, the temple will surely fall to the ground. Only solid and solid will intertwine to build a temple Divine. Your temple is a place of worship; a place to be honoured by you and all.

Thus, you may and thus you might, resist laying solid foundations in yourself and all you do. This resistance is futile and unyielding, for every time you deceive yourself of your own Divine design, you place your place in the sinking sand, the marshy land, the volatile terrain. The tumbling tower will be visible to all.

Thus, you must come to know your Divine design. You must come to know the architecture of your soul. Place your temple on a land solid and true and you will be a tower of strength, a worthy witness, a beacon, a safe keeper of your own soul.

For of Divine design you are and of Divine
design you are destined to become.

45

∞ The Mapmaker ∞

May your map fit perfectly with the map of the Divine. The Divine connects all people and placcs, so your map may have its place within the place of all that is. That you might align with the map of destiny and thus find and lose yourself in all that is. For inside you, there is a compass calibrated to the map of destiny. If thou might hear the click of precision, in which the moment comes that you might find your Self.

The mapmaker of the Divine has placed a course within your soul. If thou could know, all that is required of you, is to trust and journey forth, to find your place and purpose on the map of destiny.

The mapmaker is meticulously precise. The map drawn to scale, leads to a treasure untold. A journey for the bold. Be daring and true in your travels. Whilst on paper the journey might look complex and arduous, within you lies all that is required. You must simply trust and travel.

The Divine mapmaker has drawn the map of destiny. This is a map of magic; for once your place is found and known, a new destination of greater heights shall be revealed to you. And once again you must simply trust and travel.

Thus, it is a magic map; slightly elusive for the destination shifts. Once the treasure is found, a new promised land is revealed. You must know that once the thirst for expansion is touched and known within, one will always be the restless and unsettled

Michelle Stone

traveller. One cannot lay down true roots in one place, as the knowledge that another destination will call you forth exists.

And so, the Divine mapmaker has set forth the map of destiny for all. Within this map lies your map. Once you find your map, it will be unfolding. For as you unfold, so too will the heights to which you travel unfold. Complacency will shrivel the zest and wonder for your potential. Thus, you must not settle in any place or space in which you find yourself. Life is large and the world expansive and many experiences wait to be known. Trust and travel to the heights for which thou art calibrated for. Compass in hand and Divinity above and the traveller's question being where is my place? Where is my space?

The Divine mapmaker has placed a course within your soul.

46

∞ Your Niche ∞

Where is your place? Where are your people? Where do you belong? Who is seeking you? Where does your joy of purpose dwell? In what place or person will your potential be unleashed? Where is your fit? Where does your destiny lie? Where is your niche?

Foremost, you must effortlessly seek the Divinity within yourself. For within this place all answers are to be found. The solutions to the yearnings of your soul, your deepest desires and ideals are found within you. And when you find that place, you will know the truth of your perfect purpose and potential. Thus, the niche you so seek will be revealed to you.

For you may have considered yourself content and fulfilled in perhaps what was an abstract thought devoid of the deepest of deepest feelings. Thus, you may have thought you knew but did you truly know? For every experience, must be lived to be known. It is only as you journey forth that one experience can be compared to the ones preceding it. Thus, your understanding of you and your experiences is constantly evolving. And as you journey forth, you realise that thought was simply that: a thought and what you knew, you did not truly know.

Thus, desire with all your heart to align with your niche. As you set the purest of intentions to discover your niche, at that very moment your niche will begin seeking you. And like conspiring partners in the game of potential and purpose, your supported and supportive searching of each other will ensure that your conspiring alignment is prosperous in the revelation of you and your niche.

Thus, you must question the niche, desire the niche, and seek the niche. Be open to being discovered and more than anything else trust that the purest of intentions are always fulfilled. Life is destined to be so and you are destined to be so.

You are the niche, you seek the niche, Thy will
be done and your place revealed to you.

47

∞ The Illusion of Aloneness ∞

What could aloneness be only a space absent of connection. When you truly disconnect from yourself, only then will you experience the illusion of aloneness. Whilst you may disconnect from yourself, the Divine will never disconnect from you. Thus, you are never truly alone. You may be momentarily or periodically remiss of the Divine within and above you; nonetheless you are never truly alone. Thus, it can be said that aloneness is a mere illusion; a trick of the mind, cloaking the memory of the soul.

Aloneness is the rebuke or remiss of your oneness. Thus, aloneness is not a permanent severing of connection. Connections of the deepest and most Divine nature can never be broken. Connections can only be cloaked in veils of illusion. Thus, when the moment descends and you come to know and realise this, you know beyond shadow or veil of doubt, you are never truly alone.

The moment of realisation happens when you remind yourself or glance with hindsight on your past. You smile and as you realise that whilst your eye might not have been on the Divine, the eye of the Divine was always on you. Thus, you realise that even in your state of remiss, you were always cared for and protected. What you needed was never absent and always placed at your feet in the land in which you walked. Thus, reflections on the nature and virtue of the past can be beautifully sweet, stirring the smile above all smiles. The smile of your soul and the eye that was of the Divine is now truly brighter than ever, a twinkling diamond.

Michelle Stone

Thus, you must treasure above all treasures, the connections of a Divine nature within your life. As you sought them, they were seeking you. Those connections might continually search you and seek you within you, to reveal, enhance and edify your Divinity. Connections of this form or virtue are truly sacred and must be treated and upheld as such. Those connections cannot be broken; another's eyes will always be on you and on your back as the eye of the Divine. Thus, remember to give thanks for the presence of connections within your life. You are never truly alone; you have true people. Aloneness is an illusion.

And thus, you must and thus you might be the star who guides another's path tonight. You are of the moon and of the sun. You are of the Divine. You are and always were truly connected to all that was within, around and above you. You are truly sacred and calibrated for connection. You know that who you are and what you do has influence on another and influence on all.

Rather than an island you are a star within a galaxy.
Your place can never be taken or removed for to do so would change the beauty of the landscape in which you lie.

48

∞ The Metaphor of the Divine Fire ∞

At a particular point in a particular time, in a particular person, the moment may come for the Divine fire to blaze trails across your existence. You might have desired consciously or unknowingly for the Divine fire to commence its' journey through your existence. She must burn away all that no longer serves you, your Divinity, your becoming, your potential, and your purpose. Accordingly, all that was not Divine will be engulfed in flames and permanently transformed into Divine ashes that will nourish the seeds of your soul.

Thus, all that did not burn in the Divine fire, you must trust and treasure for these were meant to stay unharmed. They are of Divine form and purpose. As the Divine fire, blazed flames on the illusions, these same flames were reflected on the inextinguishable Divine aspects of your life. Thus, in that moment they were lit up by the burning flames and visible brighter than ever. The Divine aspects of your life are more solid than ever. They did not fall and now are thus more Divine than ever known to be.

The already Divine elements of you and your tribe connections were in the moment of the Divine fire more edified and sacrosanct than previous. They were truly holy places and people. Their place in your life was previously ordained and orchestrated, blessed and sealed by the Divine. The Divine held an impenetrable ring around them and they were untouched and sealed in your journey forth.

As you give gratitude in all things, give gratitude for the Divine fire. Whilst you do not know what will remain, trust that all that was no longer serving you will be removed. Only the Divinely approved will remain. The ashes will lay foundation for what is yet to come. The blazing removal of illusions has only created more space for you to receive and create more Divinity in a previously unyielding space of illusion. The Divine fire bequeaths a new beginning. Trust who and what are left by your side and be open and ready to receive. All that did not have a stake in your soul was removed to give way for your Divinity and the Divinity of all from this moment forth.

So, trust the path now set forth and allow all else to fall away. The Divine fire entered to bring chaos to calm. Death precedes birth. Thus, you must recognise the moment of the Divine fire and trust all that emerges from this point forward. The Divine fire only seeks to remove the blocks that impeded the emergence of your potential and purpose. The Divine fire creates a fertile space of potential.

At a particular point in a particular time,
in a particular person, the moment may come for the
Divine fire to blaze trails across your existence.

49

∞ Inner Authority ∞

Upon whom or what do you stake your faith? The government leader, the president, the priest, the minister, the psychic, the rector, the rabbi or the clairvoyant, the careless whisper? The lover, the friend, the foe, the parent? Why would you give your inner authority to another, to your destiny's end?

'Tis beguiling and bewildering that the name that you would follow would be any other than your own. Within you lies a power greater than the power of any other. You are all and all is you.

You are the home of fire. You are full of discernment, integrity, accountability, and authority. The voice to follow and the call to heed lies within you. Where and why would you betray your Self, and stake your loyalty to another before you stake your loyalty to you?

Do you really need another to be your own inner authority? Why would you not listen to you? Why would you not trust you? Although the ground upon which you walk may be shaky and broken, you are always solid within you.

Why might you require another to impart the difference between right and wrong, justice and injustice, the road to take, the path to travel?

I tell you, within you lies your own powerful inner authority. If you place the voice of another above your own, then commit this act with a heavy heart and a sense of betrayal that burdens you and expect refrain from blame. For you have betrayed yourself and placed another above you. We are all equal and equal we must stand. Rejoice in the sacred inner authority that lies in everyone. Honour the call and following of you, for he who follows his inner authority, liberates, and inspires another to do the same.

I command and commend your honouring of you. Thus, equal we stand in honouring the inner authority that is of the Divine. Although you may be broken in your humanness, you own your voice. You own your truth. You own your inner authority. From the Divine within all shall proceed. Thus, there are only winners.

The title is not the making of a man.
Your role tells me little. Your truth tells me all.

50

∞ The Art of Perfect Imperfection ∞

Can you resonate with the truth that you are a masterpiece? You are a piece of art, perfect in its imperfection. Whilst seeking perfection, you must come to know the perfection that is only found in imperfection. In this space lies perfection in its purest form. Within you lies a space of perfection; your essence, your Divinity, your soul. A place where you are not lacking or tarnished or damaged or broken. A space where you are truly perfect. All imperfection that closets this space is a mere illusion. All the failure, the misgivings, the misguided endeavours, all brokenness, all regrets of misuse of yourself and your inherent power, are illusions of your imperfections. Within you lies a most beautiful creation of perfection surrounded by imperfection. The imperfection highlights and amplifies your perfection. Thus, imperfection serves the purpose of contrasting your perfection, of making your beauty more defined and pronounced.

And as the artist's hand strikes the balance between your perfection and imperfection, this tentative and ongoing recreating is what makes you truly unique; truly you. You are truly perfect within your imperfection.

It remains a slightly wonderful and magical experience, when one speaks of their brokenness or imperfection that another only sees their perfection and beauty. Thus, you are compelled and gifted the experience of compassion and the Divine opportunity to see perfect imperfection. You see another as he truly is; the one of the One; the greatest one.

Thus, you must know that your imperfection, whilst an illusion serves that you might know your perfection. As you journey forth you redefine and recreate yourself, you break down all the light walls of imperfection and all barriers to your perfection. You come to know that a battle fought and a victory achieved within is a truly joyful experience. The illusions of imperfection will fall away effortlessly and a bright, blazing light will emanate from within you for all to see and all to know. Then with the smile of an innocent child you realise that your perfection was ever-present and all along, you were a Divine perfection within imperfection.

The truth: you are a masterpiece. All along,
you were a Divine perfection within imperfection.

51

∞ You are Ready for Love ∞

As your heart so desires, your destiny goes...the warrior's code. Thus, you are ready for the truest of all desires. You are ready to reclaim your Divine inheritance and your true birth right. By virtue of being here and reflective of your truest form, you are ready for love.

And thus, you are compelled to ask stern questions of yourself such as, what is love? When will I know, I am in love? Who will I love? Does love require compromise, settling or endurance? Where will I find the love I reverently seek? And thus, the latter question is the one from which all other questions are effortlessly answered. So where will you find the love you so reverently seek? I tell you truly that you will find this love within you. You must first be present to this love within you before you impart this love to another.

This love is designed to nourish you firstly. Your love feeds you and then another. If you trifle with this simple equation, then the elements won't combine to release Divine love.

You must stand true to you and enjoy and revel in the experience of drinking the water of your own soul. If you do not nourish your own thirst and impart your Divine drink to another, you will feel empty and depleted. So, nourish you before you nourish another.

This equation of nourishment places all elements in their truthful position where they are destined to be. Accordingly, all will flow in a Divine rhythm. The elements of the equation will recycle and replenish each other; love is an infinite cycle.

You must step into this infinite rhythm and come to know two parts feeding each other, anchoring each other, crossed and sealed by the Divine and the creed of 'I travel not without but within you. I am of love, you are of love and between us love is found. I love you not because of who you are but because of who I am. As my soul draws you near to me, I feel our holiness. I honour you as I honour me'. Of love, you came and of love you are destined to return

As my heart so desires, my destiny goes.

52

∞ Random Acts of Kindness ∞

Random acts of kindness are Divine moments of destiny. Rather than random, they are precisely chosen. Rather than acts, they are the truest undertakings. Rather than kindness they are the Divine impartment of within one to within another. As you called the Divine answered and orchestrated the moment between your heart and another's.

In that moment, you gave freely of yourself with no expectation of return. Rather than feeling lesser than you, your giving edified another. In that moment, the Divine within you was at play. You and another were more than strangers. The veil of illusion was removed and you saw another and another saw you. Perhaps, a mystery that your eyes travelled to the depths of another's soul and responded. And thus, while you saw another, the Divine overseen it all. Random acts of kindness the term of man, but the act and orchestration of the Divine.

A moment of fate will wake you up. As the light within you flashed within the briefest of encounters. In that moment, the other was ally to your soul and somehow in that moment you were edified and exalted. As through the act of another, the Divine actioned that you and another would be forever changed.

'Twas, as if you had unknowingly derailed from the train of your destiny, of Divinity. Now that train was back on track and thus you know that now you must quit standing on the platform waiting for life to begin, for now your train has arrived and thus forth you are challenged to quit waiting on the train and be the train. Make it happen...whatever is required and allow random acts of kindness to be the realignment of your soul; placing you back on track as you move increasingly towards your Divine purpose, your Divine journey, your Divine destiny.

And thus, when you are called to action by the Divine to commit a random act of kindness, do not shy away or consider it misguided or inappropriate for you to reveal love for a stranger. For in that moment you are called to be a vessel of and for the Divine. You shall come to know you and another in your truest states: states of splendour. You act on behalf of the Divine and no greater calling could ever exist. Thus, as you found and received, you gave.

Random acts of kindness:
the term of man but the act and orchestration of the Divine.

53

∞ The Well of Your Soul ∞

The well of your soul replenishes you as you drink of the Divinity within. Whilst your body may be weary and your spirit dry, the hunger and thirst of your soul is the appetite that must be satisfied. All cravings are and remain secondary to the hunger of your soul.

And thus, you must remember to drink of life and drink of you from the well of your soul. The well of your soul holds infinite water. The purest of refreshments lies in your soul, that your thirst may never go unfulfilled. You must simply allow the Divine within to replenish you.

For within, the Divine has placed fire and water. Both are of the purest form. Rather than destroying each other, these elements work in tandem so that you might reach your perfect potential. You are equipped with the necessary elements to achieve and succeed.

So, drink of your soul and be joyous and merry. Celebrate and commemorate at the greatest gathering of two, as within you the Divine above meets the Divine within at the well of your soul.

As you require the water of life, your desire is answered. Drink not in haste or slow pace but drink with a savouring of this moment of nourishment. This drinking of you, enables sober thought alone and dissolves all empty experience of drunkenness whereby you drank of life and remained unfulfilled. From the cup of this empty endeavour you were brought here to the well of your own soul.

Michelle Stone

Thus, your misguided seeking was the impetus that brought you to the well of your soul.

Once you drink of your soul and touch your spirit, you are in a state of sobriety and unequivocal clarity. And as you journey forth, you do so in knowingness that you will return repeatedly to the well of your soul for reprieve and replenishment.

> Drunken by life, you returned within. You drank
> of your cup and now you see you, another, and
> all of life. You are surely replenished.

∞ Believe ∞

A belief seeds all true and lasting transformation; a belief of the purest and truest form. A belief, things as they are can be better. A belief, that you can be better, that another can be better. Thus, you must stretch each other gently to the limits of your perfect potential. Belief is powerful and you must desire more for you and another in all things, at all times, at all costs. Sometimes one does not know the place wherein one will find himself and yet he trusts that his belief is of the truest form and that his belief and knowingness will be duly rewarded.

Many times, your brethren may have failed you, but in their essence, they have failed themselves. You must not stand idly by as your brother betrays himself, for in that place you are failing both him and you. You must discern your actions and utterances with due diligence and proceed accordingly. Seek not to punish another but rather to assist him in his own self-realisation. Thus, belief holds much responsibility and must be held with a sacredness of the soul.

Belief holds due reward. Your belief will transform you. As you declare "I know not all and not why, but I believe in a better way, a greater path and I will not compromise my own being nor will I compromise your being", then you are in a state of true honour and virtue. Thus, you are liberated. Whilst your love may hold much for yourself and another, don't ever allow another to seek that you shall become small in his presence, for in that moment you must choose the path most high and the land most Divine. You honour all of you and all of another.

Belief is birthed when you know not all but you know that *this* is not of the highest accord. And thus, you await your actions to be revealed to you and your knowingness to guide you. You align with the Divine within and around. And as you believe, you will inspire another. For the masses are hungry for the greater path and the greater way. And belief of the highest form will inspire all. As you trust, they trust and you will become the maker and keeper of the light.

Those who believe with a passion are unrelenting in their seeking and their searching. The Divine will reward their desire and their fortitude. All change and return to the intended way of being is of the highest call. One must commence in the world in which one is and believe in a greater path and a greater way. And as he changes his own world, he is mighty for he knows he can change not the world but he can change his world.

A belief seeds all true and lasting transformation; a belief of the purest and truest form. A belief, things as they are can be better.

55

∞ Taken for Granted ∞

How many times have you forgotten yourself and the essence of you and the way and the path truly Divine? How many times have you forgotten another's love and presence in your life? How many times have you failed to uphold and honour the virtue of another's being? How many times have you silently betrayed yourself and betrayed another? Alas, though you feel you must, how many times have you taken another for granted?

Whilst love may be endless, the memories of another that live on in your being are for the time that another is not in your world. Rather than the moment that is now and another is seated right in front of you. Look into another's eyes and tell not their ear but tell their heart that you have not taken them for granted. Whilst another loves you eternally, you will never allow another to compromise your sense of Self in the space that is shared between you.

And thus, if these words resonate with you and your experiences, how humble human will you choose to act from this point forth? Are you the knowing or unknowing perpetrator or victim or both? How will you walk the enlightened path, if walking means that another cannot come with you? Are you strong enough to be a change maker, truth seeker, destiny embracer? Will you test the mettle within and around and gracefully seek the honour within and around? Are you of integrity and are you capable of holding all parts of yourself?

Michelle Stone

You must denounce and renounce all that is not sacred, all that no longer serves you and another. You need to honour the sacred within and between you. This might be a lofty task, but of the sacred you were born and of the sacred you were destined to be.

If you truly believe that you are on borrowed time, then when is the moment when you start to live and start to love truly? You must ask these honest questions of yourself and another. You must be alone with you and seek within the times, peoples, and places where you have taken you and another for granted. You must first honour the virtue of your own being before you can honour that of another.

You must give truly of yourself in all things,
places, and spaces. Cherish you and cherish the virtue
that is you, take nothing for granted…least of all, you.

56

∞ Grief ∞

Whilst the heart knows and love truly is your birth right, rather than your love being found in only the joyous experiences and memories, your love may be found in the grief within. It is as if a space within your heart is solely reserved for grief. The tears of your eyes reveal the desires of your soul. Oh, how you grieve for another, now that he is no longer by your side. The space of love, you held within for another is now contracting. Now you feel pain, where once your love for another lay. And whilst the knower within knew that you and another would leave each other, now he is gone and the love within is painful. Melding another into memory is a wrenching process. And whilst you knew that your starting would end in parting, now you are forlorn without the other.

You grieve not another; you grieve the love untold, the yearnings unrevealed and the deepest parts you kept concealed. And thus, as these words touch your being and touch your essence, my friend, my fellow Avatar, you know the love to which I speak.

Grieving is a process wherein one's love for self and or another is melded into a new love. As you loved another then and as you love you now, you will witness your own pain, as your love for another becomes anew. In the melding process, you are the tormentor and tormented...pain, pain, pain. Melding another into memory is painful and yet priceless. If you allow your love to meld another into a graceful memory, their love will lie within you eternally. Thus, another will live on within you. Your love is another's love; they showed you all you took for granted. And you will rebirth your being anew in honour of another and in honour of you. Of the Divine you were and of the Divine you were destined to return and of the Divine you will forever hold another in your heart.

May another's absence compel and inspire you, to renew your Destiny, to revitalise your being and to live your life to your perfect potential. May you trust in the hand of the Divine that took another home. The same hand of the Divine will resurrect you from the place of pain to the space of gain. For you loved another and their absence will take you forth and you will learn to treasure the land in which you walk, to sanctify and edify yourself. You will be triumphant as you learn who you are in the absence of another. For all you found in another will now lie within you. Their gifts are yours to uncover.

Thus, you have learned to hold firm, when your love contracts into grief. You know that your love will be born anew and you were never destined to be without the other. The melding process that is grief, will distil a new love from your once felt love. It will purify the very essence of your being. The other taught you not how to die, they taught you how to live. How could one ever gift another in such a profound way?

I was taken home and I left my legacy in you…
I love you.

∞ Love ∞

Love was and remains the true nature of man. By the hand and act of the Divine he was formed and within him lies a Divine spark. The ache of the soul remains. The desperate and yet non-disparaging beating desire to be seen, known, accepted, and truly loved within the world. The space within knows that this potential exists and yet he does not heed the call of his own soul. Imprisoned within, mirroring the land in which he dwells, for the world is imprisoned by misguided assumptions, out-dated beliefs, erroneous thinking, impure concepts, and limited awareness of the virtue of man and the virtue of all. It remains…of love you are and of love you are destined to become.

Man's greatest misguided act possibly has been to deny witness to the core of his own being, to not believe in his own potential to see and be seen and to set forth his actions from his mind rather than his heart. The world may be bleak and perhaps unrelentingly fake, yet the glimpse of love can still be found. The power of the moment birthed of love, is most powerful in lifting the state of man from a space of mindlessness to Divinity. And whilst the world around may be imprisoned by illusions, the moments of love are real and solid. The truest moments, edify the human spirit and honour the Divinity of one and all.

Love is a Divine energy. Unfortunately, man has contorted and twisted his limited understanding around this Divine energy and thus imprisoned the essence of his being. Around his essence, his defences lie and what cannot come in cannot be released: love. And thus, man must set him free from himself. He must find his essence, know his essence and be his essence. Then he will be *spiritual.* Love is a Divine energy and thus can only be felt. It is the force that can break through the invisible walls and unnecessary defences and touch your soul. Love is not of the mind; love is of the soul. Love is thus, beyond definition.

The journey to love is perhaps, man's greatest mystery and yet man's greatest potential. For in the essence of his being, he knows it exists and simultaneously he knows that he is unsure of where it might be found or what it may look like. Thus, he searches for it in the presence of another, in the arms of a lover, in the unintended interaction, the face of a child or the land in which he dwells. He is relentless in his seeking without for what lies within. All people, places and encounters hold the potential for one to feel love. Around you may show you what lies within you. Love is not outside you, it is within you.

Love is everywhere and within one and all. Thus, you must examine the limits that you have set upon love; the abstractions of your mind where the limit to your love lies. You search for love in another and yet he is too old, too young, not quite right, and inadequate, of the wrong mind or of the wrong making. Yet, your connection to him may be so strong that you feel you can't ignore it. And yet you think...you think... you think. Thus, the mind guides your actions and love is not of the mind. The heart truly knows...

Love cannot be differentiated into strong and weak, only connection can. Love is found in moments and cannot be segregated by relationship. The moment of love you feel with your lover may be as strong as the moment you share with another.

The lover's task is to offer you repeated moments of love, to make moments of love, to make memories of love that nourish your soul and replenish your spirit. The repeated opportunity for you to feel the Divinity within, to find your love, for love is not given from one to another. Rather the moment resonates with your love within, it is always within you.

Man, reverently desires to see and to be seen, to see another behold his Divinity, to see another reflect his essence back to him. The moments where his essence is not truly reflected to him can cause the erroneous thought and belief, that he is unworthy. Thus, man must firstly reveal himself to himself. He must set himself free from himself. He must see himself as he truly is...Divine.

Man, must allow his heart to guide his actions.
His being unmanaged by his mind, he will see and be seen.
He will be of love, of love he is and of
love he is destined to become.

58

∞ Rule the World ∞

You rule the world that is your own: a land of richness, a land of virtue, a land of toil, a land of spoil, a land of integrity, a land of truth, a land of love. You are a land and love Divine. Yes, you rule the world in which you dwell.

In every given moment, you are receptive. You receive all that another and the world desires to feed you. You see beauty within you. You see beauty in the sky above you. Another nourishes and nurtures you. As the rose surely blossoms, you are destined to open and become the delicate being that is you. If you detach from the Source of your being, then surely it follows that you will shrivel and die like the rose separated from the earth. Thus, you must choose to rule the world in which you dwell, by remaining connected to you, another and the Source that feeds you both. You rule the world.

You are the warden of your own soul and thus admittance is within your remit. What you observe is your right. Do you see death or rebirth, complexity or simplicity, suffering or survival, darkness or light, the present or the absent, abundance or lack, the illusions or the truth, the fear or the love?

You rule the world and thus, like all rulers you hold influence. You can direct your destiny, you call and you are answered, you seek and you behold. The way you direct your influence reflects you. To where and to whom do you invest your Self? From where is your knowledge and wisdom derived? From whom do you seek your counsel? Who directs your faith and your knowingness of justice?

In all things and tasks, be wise to the depths of you. Behold your own creativity, for you must invest your gifts and talents in alignment with your purpose. Channel yourself wisely. Your finite existence compels you to engage in measured deliberation and discerned action. Remember of the Divine you are and as the Divine is the ruler of all that is, within you a Divine ruler is found. Remember, you rule the world in which you dwell.

Rule the world: pour yourself forth wisely.

59

∞ Of Love, you are ∞

Of love, you are and of love you are destined to return. The stars of the sky lie within you. You are of the moon and sun. The light inside you casts out all shadows and penetrates all veils of illusion. You are in your natural state of being; you are in love.

The cloak of life may cover your Self; shroud your soul. Whilst dimming your light, this cloak may never extinguish it. You may have cloaked your soul to protect the light within you. Thus, this cloak has served you well.

Now that you do possess infinite confidence in your light, the preserving cloak has vanished. Now, you are a magician of sorts, thrusting this cloak effortlessly and graciously to reveal, the magical reappearance of your soul. You are the magician of truth, removing the cloak of illusion to reveal the beauty of truth. As magic lies within you, you see magic all around you.

By the hand of magic, you were derived and by the hand of magic you will be known from this day forth. You are of love and love alone and by love you will reside. You were wise in the cloaking of your soul, as you knew the precious needed protection. Thus, you protected the love within until you came of age. The defenceless is now the defender, the protected now the protector.

You brought you from a place of fear to a space of love. Of love, you are and of love you were destined to return. 'Tis so, because the Divine declared it to be so. Now of age, you can behold the light within and only be of love.

Of love, you are and of love you are destined to return.

60

∞ The Alchemist Within ∞

You are an alchemist and within you lies the power to transform, to transmute, to breakdown, to dissolve, to distil and to blend. You take what was the breaking of you and allow it to be the making of you. You turn lead into gold. Of gold, you are and of gold you are destined to return.

You are the practitioner of alchemy. Within you, you find all you desire and all you are destined to become. You find the answer to every mystery. You dissolve the darkness to bring forth the light. You distil every challenge, every so-called failure, every wrong and all wrong doing done to you. You break all life events down and in breaking them open, you behold a light bright. You rework your history to reveal an inner mystery.

You know all that serves you and all that no longer serves you is transmuted. All your mistruths birth your truths. You blend, you break, you make. All that you thought you knew and every misguided adventure becomes the solid foundation from which you thrust yourself forth.

For all, whom trust in the process of alchemy, Divinity is assured. Thus, you must allow what comes forth from within you, you must search and seek within to find its rightful resting place. You must question to whom does this mistake or virtue belong? All that is not of you must be placed in the simmering pot, to distil all that is… only you.

You must only be, you in your rawest and purest state and

destiny is yours to make. Be only of you and only in you. You must take the alchemist's journey to discover the sacred soul that is… You. Although lead may be where you start, gold is the place from where you will depart. You are priceless. Of gold, you are and of gold you are destined to return.

Within you the alchemist lies.

∞ The Gap ∞

In the utterances of your mouth and mind you profess yourself to be kind, well intentioned, loving, and spiritual. I want to know the expressions of your soul. I want to know and see the depths of you made manifest in the world.

I truly declare to you, that between the utterances of your mouth and your way manifest in the world, a gap is found. If you could acknowledge this gap between the utterances of your mouth and your actions, you would find the birthing space of your way forth.

For whilst you do declare who you are, I need you to show me who you are. If you tell me, you are spiritual, tell me sternly how this is made visible and vivid in the world you walk. For if you decline to show up in your life and live the decrees of your soul, then your life and being shall remain hollow and your perfect potential unfulfilled.

You told me, you were many things and of many ways and yet you could not truly believe it. For you recognised the gapping gap between thoughts, self-concepts, abstract notions of yourself and your actual experiencing and actual engagement with the world.

Thus, it remains, the gapping gap within you that causes you also to remain unknown to yourself, another, and the world. Try as you may and try as you might to not betray yourself and another…you do.

I see the gap and I see your pain. You must sit in the gap,

for your being in the gap, will birth you forth. The space of incongruence will become one of congruence as you meld your word with your way. You will move forward surefooted and solid in you and in your way. You will know of what you are and what you are not. You will know your words and choose to reveal your Self in truth as you are and know your Self to be; Divine.

There will be no grieving when you leave this existence, for you will have lived a life of oneness with your Self. You came, you were and you will live on.

The gap between your word and your way, will birth you.

62

∞ Vulnerability ∞

When one realises the littleness of all that he is, vulnerability arises. Vulnerability is a broken state; one is broken by life and broken by his own limited understanding. In the eyes of the Divine, he is of unlimited potential and purpose; he is an infinite being. Yet, he is the human who knows little and desires to know all. How does man reconcile the Avatar within with the human that shows him where his limits are? How does he become Avatar alone?

Man becomes Avatar alone when he realises that he is Avatar alone. Whilst the human and the Avatar within may battle and be in opposition to another, the Avatar is greater. The human mind could never understand all, but the Avatar can be all. Man, must realise and release the human experience repeatedly as he moves into his Avatar greatness. He must desire more than anything else his own greatness and accordingly diminish his own littleness. Hiding your understanding from yourself and another only creates pain, so why would you repeatedly engage in this process of betrayal of yourself?

Thus, you must allow the walls around you to crash down and recognise within yourself the human who desires for all to remain the same, for safety is found for the human in the known and not the unknown. The human grapples and desires to apply human concepts and understanding to Divine precedence for he believes that if his littleness is made known, he will cease to exist, yet this moment of profound vulnerability will only precede his rise to greatness.

Thus, you must recognise the human resisting the Avatar within. Recognise and realise your identification with this being to become an entity of greatness. Realise and release your human mind that desires to hide your splendour and allow the Avatar of brilliance within to be made manifest. Remember this process will be akin to losing a skin, you will lose one way of being that has served you well and whilst not always pleasant, the human brought you thus far and deserves to be honoured.

You will grieve for the human that you thought was you, but remember you grieve not the life that was lived, you grieve the realisation that every moment prior to the Avatar way was incomplete; in realising your completeness then and only then will you recognise your previous incompleteness, and this may be a painful realisation to navigate. Thus, you must hold yourself sacred throughout this tender and tumultuous process. During this process, you will be in a state of agitation, you will be unsettled and thus you must remember that it is only in this state of unsettlement that growth is possible; one must be unsettled to grow. The soil around the rose plant must be agitated to facilitate emergence of the rose and similarly agitation is prerequisite for your growth.

Finally, as you grieve the human experience and step fully into the Avatar way, know that life holds many blessings and truths for you. You are being born not anew, for the Avatar always lay within you, rather you are becoming the being that you were destined to be, you are Avatar and your greatest desire is being fulfilled...

Man's greatest desire was and remains to see and be seen in the totality and truth of all that he is; truly Divine. He is of Divine purpose, potential and nature. Man desires not a miracle but rather a world in which he can truly be free: to love and to be loved.

63

∞ The Sacred Secret ∞

The Avatar revealed that they time was nigh for his departure and he held one final declaration. He proclaimed, "You who has recorded my word, write this…"

You are not human…

I am Avatar ∞ You are Avatar.

∞∞∞∞∞∞∞∞∞